Günter Grass

T0345546

Titles in the series Critical Lives present the work of leading cultural figures of the modern period. Each book explores the life of the artist, writer, philosopher or architect in question and relates it to their major works.

In the same series

Antonin Artaud *David A. Shafer*
Roland Barthes *Andy Stafford*
Georges Bataille *Stuart Kendall*
Charles Baudelaire *Rosemary Lloyd*
Simone de Beauvoir *Ursula Tidd*
Samuel Beckett *Andrew Gibson*
Walter Benjamin *Esther Leslie*
John Berger *Andy Merrifield*
Leonard Bernstein *Paul R. Laird*
Joseph Beuys *Claudia Mesch*
Jorge Luis Borges *Jason Wilson*
Constantin Brancusi *Sanda Miller*
Bertolt Brecht *Philip Glahn*
Charles Bukowski *David Stephen Calonne*
Mikhail Bulgakov *J.A.E. Curtis*
William S. Burroughs *Phil Baker*
John Cage *Rob Haskins*
Albert Camus *Edward J. Hughes*
Fidel Castro *Nick Caistor*
Paul Cézanne *Jon Kear*
Coco Chanel *Linda Simon*
Noam Chomsky *Wolfgang B. Sperlich*
Jean Cocteau *James S. Williams*
Salvador Dalí *Mary Ann Caws*
Guy Debord *Andy Merrifield*
Claude Debussy *David J. Code*
Gilles Deleuze *Frida Beckman*
Fyodor Dostoevsky *Robert Bird*
Marcel Duchamp *Caroline Cros*
Sergei Eisenstein *Mike O'Mahony*
Gustave Flaubert *Anne Green*
Michel Foucault *David Macey*
Mahatma Gandhi *Douglas Allen*
Jean Genet *Stephen Barber*
Allen Ginsberg *Steve Finbow*
Günter Grass *Julian Preece*
Ernest Hemingway *Verna Kale*
Derek Jarman *Michael Charlesworth*
Alfred Jarry *Jill Fell*
James Joyce *Andrew Gibson*

Carl Jung *Paul Bishop*
Franz Kafka *Sander L. Gilman*
Frida Kahlo *Gannit Ankori*
Søren Kierkegaard *Alastair Hannay*
Yves Klein *Nuit Banai*
Arthur Koestler *Edward Saunders*
Akira Kurosawa *Peter Wild*
Lenin *Lars T. Lih*
Jean-François Lyotard *Kiff Bamford*
Stéphane Mallarmé *Roger Pearson*
Gabriel García Márquez *Stephen M. Hart*
Karl Marx *Paul Thomas*
Henry Miller *David Stephen Calonne*
Herman Melville *Kevin J. Hayes*
Yukio Mishima *Damian Flanagan*
Eadweard Muybridge *Marta Braun*
Vladimir Nabokov *Barbara Wyllie*
Pablo Neruda *Dominic Moran*
Georgia O'Keeffe *Nancy J. Scott*
Octavio Paz *Nick Caistor*
Pablo Picasso *Mary Ann Caws*
Edgar Allan Poe *Kevin J. Hayes*
Ezra Pound *Alec Marsh*
Marcel Proust *Adam Watt*
John Ruskin *Andrew Ballantyne*
Jean-Paul Sartre *Andrew Leak*
Erik Satie *Mary E. Davis*
Arthur Schopenhauer *Peter B. Lewis*
Adam Smith *Jonathan Conlin*
Susan Sontag *Jerome Boyd Maunsell*
Gertrude Stein *Lucy Daniel*
Igor Stravinsky *Jonathan Cross*
Pyotr Tchaikovsky *Philip Ross Bullock*
Leon Trotsky *Paul Le Blanc*
Richard Wagner *Raymond Furness*
Simone Weil *Palle Yourgrau*
Tennessee Williams *Paul Ibell*
Ludwig Wittgenstein *Edward Kanterian*
Virginia Woolf *Ira Nadel*
Frank Lloyd Wright *Robert McCarter*

Günter Grass

Julian Preece

REAKTION BOOKS

In memoriam Stephen Hayward

Published by Reaktion Books Ltd
Unit 32, Waterside
44–48 Wharf Road
London N1 7UX, UK

www.reaktionbooks.co.uk

First published 2018
Copyright © Julian Preece 2018

Printed and bound in Great Britain by Bell & Bain, Glasgow

A catalogue record for this book is available from the British Library

ISBN 978 1 78023 901 9

Contents

Prologue: Many-sided Man 7

1 From Danzig to Paris, 1927–59: Living *The Tin Drum*   17

2 Art and Violence in the Early Fiction 53

3 Public Uses of Fame: Willy Brandt and the SPD 77

4 Back to the Future, Forward to the Past 99

5 Crying Wolf in 'Orwell's Decade'? 122

6 Learning to Love the Berlin Republic: *Too Far Afield* 144

7 The New Nation Is Me 158

8 The Culmination of Project Self 173

Epilogue: Poetry and Death 194

References 198

Select Bibliography 214

Acknowledgements 221

Photo Acknowledgements 222

Günter Grass at an exhibition of his artworks in the Gallery Schürer (Switzerland), December 1982. Behind him: the lithograph 'Horn-rimmed Pike' from the Father's Day Cycle and the copperplate etching 'Two Crayfish on Pebbles'.

Prologue: Many-sided Man

The memorial celebration at Lübeck Theatre on 10 May 2015 to celebrate the life of Günter Grass, who had died at the age of 87 the previous month, was broadcast live on German Sunday afternoon television. Flags flew at half-mast in Schleswig-Holstein, where Grass had lived for the last thirty years, just outside the village of Behlendorf next to the canal which connects the Elbe and Trave rivers. Guest of honour at the celebration was federal president Joachim Gauck, a former dissident pastor in the German Democratic Republic and chairman of the commission dealing with the legacy of the Stasi. He was flanked by ex-chancellor Gerhard Schröder, a close friend and political confidant of the deceased. Also present were current deputy chancellor Sigmar Gabriel, Paweł Adamowicz, the city president of Gdańsk, where Grass was born when it was still called Danzig, alongside the mayor of Hamburg and the first ministers of Schleswig-Holstein and North Rhine Westphalia. In her opening address, Monika Grütters, minister of culture in Angela Merkel's government, predicted that Grass's work would sit next to Goethe's in the German tradition. Apart from Gauck (an independent) and the Christian Democrat Grütters, the politicians present were Social Democrats, representatives of Germany's oldest political party, the SPD (Sozial-Demokratische Partei Deutschlands), which Grass supported tirelessly in election campaigns and celebrated in his fiction for more than half a century.

Speeches by politicians alternated with Grass poems: 'Despite Everything', from his most recent volume *Mayflies*, affirmed his love of Germany and could almost have been written for the occasion; the valedictory 'I Dreamt I Had to Take My Leave', from his once controversial novel *The Rat*, was recited by his daughter Helene Grass; and, finally, Mario Adorf, who played Alfred Matzerath in the Oscar-winning film of his first and most famous novel, *The Tin Drum*, read the autobiographical 'Kleckerburg', written at the same time as the Danzig fiction which first made its author famous.

According to the television announcer, Grass cited three reasons for moving to Lübeck: 'Danzig, Thomas Mann and Willy Brandt'. The city's redbrick Gothic architecture reminded him of his native city, another Hanseatic port which was the mainspring of his fiction – of his major works only *Too Far Afield* and *Grimms' Words* do not connect directly with Danzig/Gdańsk on his beloved Baltic Sea. Thomas Mann (1875–1955), the greatest German novelist of the twentieth century and the most powerful German voice in the struggle against Nazism, set his first and most famous novel *Buddenbrooks* in Lübeck, though without mentioning the city by name. Grass emulates the feint in the opening two chapters of *The Tin Drum* by coyly delaying naming Danzig. Like Mann, Grass remained fascinated by artist figures from the German past, though it was more their interactions with power than their place in the cultural canon which concerned him. When Grass took to the campaign trail in 1965 on behalf of Willy Brandt (1913–1992), another native Lübecker, he cited Walt Whitman on democracy (IX:99), as Mann did in his seminal address 'On the German Republic' in 1922.[1] Brandt was an anti-Nazi resister who returned from Scandinavian exile in 1945 to set about transforming Germany into a democratic state. For Grass, Brandt embodied both the 'better Germany' and the spirit of gradualist reformism which he would make his own. Mann, Brandt and Grass now all have museums in Lübeck dedicated to their life and work a stone's throw from each other.

On 10 May 2015, however, it was an American novelist who delivered the eulogy to Günter Grass. In contrast to the more earnest German and Polish contributions, John Irving, a literary imitator who became a friend, radiated charm and made jokes. Speaking mainly in English, he recalled that in the early 1960s his Viennese landlady was shocked to see the visiting student from the USA arrive home with a copy of *The Tin Drum*. Irving ended by comparing his own sense of loss at Grass's death with Oskar Matzerath's reaction in *The Tin Drum* to the suicide of toyshop owner Sigismund Markus, who had supplied him hitherto with his all-important drums:

> 'There was once a toy merchant, his name was Markus, and he took all the toys in the world away with him out of this world.' I know how Oskar feels. Günter Grass was the *king* of the toy merchants.[2]

As Irving points out, Markus was Jewish and Oskar's lament is uttered in response to the November Pogrom or Kristallnacht of 1938, which prompted Markus to take his own life. In media reports of the memorial celebration, 'the great American writer' received star billing and his eulogy was reprinted in translation.[3] Seventy years – almost to the day – after the defeat of Nazism and a quarter of a century after reunification, the Berlin Republic still craved international confirmation and borrowed stardust from the major victor in that war.

Through his worldwide fame, which culminated in his winning the Nobel Prize in Literature in 1999, Günter Grass provided such confirmation in abundance. Bursting onto the literary scene at the age of 31, just four years after Mann's death, with a first novel the whole world soon wanted to read, Grass became a public institution and remained the leading writer in the language for more than half a century, his name synonymous above all with unabashed candour in addressing the Nazi past of his youth. He reflected in his writing on his failure to ask questions about the shooting of his Polish uncle Frantizek and the disappearances of classmates and teachers or simply to think through what was going on around him. As an adult he made good the mistakes he made in his youth and resolved never again to hold his tongue. Grass showed time and time again how he could grab public attention, sometimes with a play, a novel or a poem, but equally often with a gesture or statement which left no doubt which side he took on a question of moment. In the modern era writers have played such roles at times of national self-doubt by representing a certain idea of what their nation should be. Victor Hugo in France, W. B. Yeats in Ireland and Adam Mickiewicz in Poland all achieved such recognition in the nineteenth or early twentieth centuries. Grass was a different case because as a supporter of the SPD, he was overtly partisan; he polarized opinion and had distinct ideas about the direction that Germany should be taking. At the peak of his powers he played the media like no other operator in public life. In the 1960s he wanted to smash the complacency which pervaded the young Federal Republic, especially, in his view, as it was concentrated in the personality of its first chancellor, Konrad Adenauer. Grass held that Adenauer's anti-communism cemented German division and found his employment of ex-Nazis in prominent positions shameful. Over the years Grass addressed other topics, such as developing-world poverty, about which he encouraged Brandt to accept the World Bank's invitation to write a pioneering report,[4] asylum, attitudes to minorities and, in the 1980s, the nuclear arms race. Running through his essays, however, like a red thread are arguments about Germany, national division and oppression in the communist East up to 1989, and the character of post-Wall, post-Auschwitz Germany thereafter. His three most significant novels, *The Tin Drum*, *The Flounder* and *Too Far Afield*, can all be read as national allegories. Grass's most controversial decision was to oppose reunification in 1990 in favour of a confederation of two German states, which he had been advocating since the days of Adenauer.

More important than his speeches and essays, but often linked closely with them, is his literary writing, produced over precisely sixty years, from *The Advantages of the Wind Chickens* in 1956, to *Of All That Ends*, which appeared four months after his death. Grass wrote a set of novels and works of shorter fiction – *erzählungen* and novellas, a volume of interconnected short stories, as well as narrative essays mixed with autobiography and poems – which contrived to be serious and popular, challenging and funny. Accompanying artwork was always integral to their conception and presentation. Up to *The Flounder* in 1977 he often calculated that some of the contents would shock. While his books were often discussed in news bulletins and once even mentioned in the Bundestag on account of their content he endeavoured to be formally innovative in each, varying the narrative conceits of the last while anticipating those of the next. Up to *The Rat* in 1986, he unfolded an oeuvre which was present *in nuce* in his imagination from the start. In the second half of his career he largely searched out new material or drew on his rich experience.

Grass was determined from a very young age to be an artist. The only question was what sort. His talent was recognized by all around him and multifaceted. Husband to the dancer Anna Schwarz from 1954 to 1978 and the musician Ute Grunert from 1979 to his death, a prolific poet, trained monumental mason and graduate in sculpture, and a student jazz musician turned avant-garde playwright who worked to the highest standards in a variety of graphic media (etchings, lithographs, charcoal, ink and watercolour), he discovered by his late twenties that he needed to become a master of prose fiction if he was to become famous. Having achieved both fame and financial independence shortly after he turned thirty, he worked hard to retain his reputation, touring the country to read from each new book, and to put his renown to good use. After the lonely months of writing, he enjoyed the interaction with readers, but the tours generated sales, kept his name in the lights and were an essential component in a unique one-man literary enterprise. In his last two decades, he recorded most of his major works to CD, performing extracts from several of them in concert halls and theatres with the percussionist Günter 'Baby' Sommer. Authors are not usually the best readers of their own works, but as a practised public orator Grass perfected this aspect of his repertoire. He wrote his prose to be heard as well as read, reciting each sentence back to himself as he committed it to paper, musicality and rhythm being as important as sense and syntax.

Grass's literary writing, however beautifully crafted, was always meant to make his readers see the world afresh. Indeed, that was usually the point of it. His political speeches were also literary performances, in which he often presented himself as the leading character in a drama, a hapless author or misunderstood citizen celebrity battling against the odds to get his voice heard. Following Albert Camus, he saw himself as Sisyphus, happily doing the right thing by rolling his rock to the top of the mountain, even if it had no apparent effect, but ready to celebrate every moment of progress.

Grass was present in the public arena in a variety of ways. He funded literary and artistic prizes which he called after his teachers and role models (the Alfred Döblin Prize for young writers in 1978; the Daniel Chodowiecki Prize for Polish creative artists in 1992). In 1985 he donated his house in Wewelsfleth to the city of Berlin for use as a writers' refuge. He sponsored the Foundations for the Roma People (1997, which awards the Otto Pankok Prize), for the writer Wolfgang Koeppen (together with fellow poet, Peter Rühmkorf, 2000), and for the SPD's first leader, August Bebel (2010, which also awards a biannual prize). He supported dissident writers across the world and sought out colleagues' company by organizing writers' meetings in emulation of Hans Werner Richter's legendary Gruppe 47 – in East Berlin in the mid-1970s, for example, or in Lübeck in the last decade of his life. The Gruppe 47, which he attended from 1955 until its last meeting in 1967, was Grass's substitute university.[5] It taught him that writers could help each other with their shared craft, as he was mentored to write *The Tin Drum*, as well as raise the public profile of their profession by demonstrating common purpose. Until ill health impeded his movements, Grass also travelled abroad, not just to promote his own books but to intervene on behalf of colleagues and make the case for the freedom of expression. National newspapers assigned dedicated Grass correspondents to accompany this unique instrument of German soft power and cultural diplomacy.

Grass was in turn feted and won just about every prize the world had to offer. In 2007, on his eightieth birthday, president Horst Köhler addressed an official event in Lübeck Theatre; the national broadcaster aired a ninety-minute documentary showing him going about his business over the preceding twelve months.[6] The first collected edition of his works appeared when he turned sixty in 1987 and was followed by two more collected editions on his next round birthdays in 1997 and 2007. These are due for completion in 2019 with the last volumes of notes and appendices. At the Jacobs University in Bremen, the Medienarchiv Günter Grass Foundation has digitized more than 2,000 of his appearances on radio and television. His correspondence between 1960 and 2006 fills 199 ringbinders, his business dealings a further 74, all catalogued at the Akademie der Künste in Berlin, which took possession of his papers in the early 2000s. There have been major biographies by Volker Neuhaus, who also edited two of the collected editions, and by Michael Jürgs, former chief editor of *Stern* magazine, whose previous subjects included the film star Romy Schneider.[7] A third by Harro Zimmermann was published in 2017 to coincide with what would have been Grass's ninetieth birthday.[8]

Yet Grass was never universally respected or accepted. From the mid-1960s, reviewers already harked back to *The Tin Drum* to find his new books disappointing. Through the 1980s he identified with a series of seemingly more extreme positions, lecturing his compatriots in ways which some took to be loftily superior; in 1995, on the publication of his novel of reunification *Too Far Afield*, there began a series of attempts in the media to destroy his reputation. Press reactions to the novel and the subsequent discussion of them filled a medium-sized book.[9] They did so again in 1997 after a speech expressing shame at his country's record on arms sales to repressive regimes, in particular to Turkey as it repressed its Kurdish minority, who in turn no longer qualified for asylum in Germany.[10] There were two further major scandals: in 2006, when he revealed that he was recruited as a sixteen-year-old to the Waffen-ss rather than to the Wehrmacht, as everyone hitherto assumed, and in 2012, after the poem 'What Has to Be Said', which decried German arms sales to Israel on the grounds that Israel could launch a nuclear strike on Iran. Again his publishers deemed that the affairs warranted documentation.[11] Grass made readable copy and watchable television, but, as a freelance author rather than political office-holder, nobody could force his resignation when he contradicted himself or appeared hypocritical. He knew how to exploit the media (at least in its pre-digital forms), but he was not their creation. He was also unelected – the only office he ever held was the presidency of the Berlin Academy of Arts in the mid-1980s – and his platform was made from that least tangible of substances: prestige. Grass's ss secret was so shocking because it contradicted the image which the broader public had cultivated of him, though it was easy to forget that he had never made any secret of his teenage enthusiasm for the Nazis.

To some degree, too, Grass outlived his times. Committed writers were associated with the era of the social-liberal coalition between 1969 and 1982, first under Brandt, then Helmut Schmidt.

Not everybody in Germany was ready to grant them a permanent place in the constitution. Grass's heroic period as a campaigning literary celebrity was the latter half of the 1960s, when he toured the country, explaining to voters how they should 'dare more democracy', according to Brandt's central slogan (which Grass may or may not have written for him). His contribution in 1990 could have been as vital, when he first argued against the immediate unification of the two German states, then against the manner in which the West swallowed up the East. The difference was that this time he acted on his own, without a convincing plan, and he found himself quickly outmanoeuvred by events, voters and the chancellor, Helmut Kohl.

Major publications about Grass in the last decade of his life, as he memorialized himself in a trio of autobiographical books, were both monumental and testament to his having lived his professional life in public from his early thirties. In 2006 Harro Zimmermann paraphrased Hölderlin in the title of his 500-page account of press reports on Grass's writing and public role: *Günter Grass among the Germans: A Chronicle*.[12] Timm Niklas Pietsch's study of his essays and speeches, which themselves stretch to more than 2,000 pages and take in a variety of genres, starting with a public letter against the building of the Berlin Wall in August 1961, is equally exhaustive and appeared the same year.[13] Grass's publishers produced a bilingual catalogue raisonné of his etchings and lithographs in two enormous volumes in 2007, edited by Grass's full-time secretary, Hilke Ohsoling.[14] The 700 pages of Stasi files reporting on him from 1961 to 1989 (plus more than 2,000 others in which his name appears) were summarized in 2010 by Kai Schlüter, showing the refusenik of reunification to have been a tireless advocate of freedom of expression in the GDR and of the cultural unity of the German nation.[15] Grass's correspondence with Willy Brandt documents an even more extraordinary association.[16] Running to more than 1,200 pages, the letters underline Grass's remarkable command of policy detail, preparedness to concentrate on the least poetic of topics, and his often original take on contemporary affairs, which Chancellor Brandt gave every sign of taking seriously. In Gdańsk, which made him an honorary citizen in 1993, there are statues of two of his most famous characters, Oskar Matzerath, the narrator of *The Tin Drum*, and Tulla Pokriefke, who plays a central role in *Cat and Mouse*, *Dog Years* and *Crabwalk*. They were joined by Grass himself shortly after his death. In the Grass House in Lübeck you can buy memorabilia as well as artwork and bronzes costing thousands of euros. Grass worked purposefully on his legacy, preparing beautiful editions of several of his books with the art publisher Gerhard Steidl, such as the belated illustrations for *Dog Years* on his second novel's fiftieth anniversary in 2013, and updating his sumptuously produced 'studio reports' in 1991, 2001 and 2014.

There are many ways to approach the life and work of Günter Grass – poet, artist, politician and writer – and it is impossible to do justice to all of them in a book of this length. I will try instead to concentrate on two central aspects: his prose fiction, which is the reason he found readers outside the German-speaking world, and his public role, which for the most part is a German affair.

1

From Danzig to Paris, 1927–59: Living *The Tin Drum*

Günter Grass was born into the maelstrom of twentieth-century European history on 16 October 1927, nine years after the end of one world war and twelve years before the start of the next – which began moreover within his very earshot in Danzig Bay. The independent, German-speaking city-state of Danzig was a largely unwanted by-product of the Treaty of Versailles, which was imposed on Germany in 1919. By the time Grass was five and a half years old, Adolf Hitler was the Reichskanzler in Berlin and his National Socialist German Workers' Party (NSDAP) was also in control of Danzig. The young Günter soon joined the designated mass organizations for boys of his age, first the Jungvolk, then the Hitlerjugend, while his father, the shopkeeper Wilhelm Grass, became a party member because it was good for business and he wanted to be part of history.

Danzig was a maritime and frontier city, its historic centre built by German colonists who arrived in advance of the Teutonic Knights who would rule for a century and a half in the late Middle Ages, suppressing the Slavic population. Situated on the delta of the mighty Vistula, which bifurcates contemporary Poland, Danzig became one of the wealthiest players in the customs and trading alliance known as the Hanseatic League, which linked ports along the North Sea and Baltic coasts. Danzig's heathen origins, as Grass relates in *The Flounder*, lasted until Bishop Adalbert of Prague was killed by locals resisting his Christian message in 997. With his murder, which merited his canonization and a written martyr's life, Danzig enters history.[1] The city's evolving demographic mix matched its rich history of conflict, forever alternating its allegiance between rival German and Polish potentates. Its least happy period, in Grass's account, was under Prussia in the nineteenth century.

Witnessing its destruction in 1945 (as Grass himself did not), the narrator and anti-hero of *The Tin Drum*, Oskar Matzerath, turns its violent past into a never-ending sequence of conquest and plunder, each invader making 'a little fire here and there' (III:520) before being repelled or settling down to govern for a while. Grass absorbed this history as a child and drew on it in his fiction. His first attempt at creative writing while still a schoolboy was a medieval romance set among the Cassubians, a tribal group neither German nor Polish who live mainly on the urban periphery, which he submitted to a Hitlerjugend writing competition. Luckily for his future reputation, so he reflected in 1980 in *Headbirths*, he did not win a prize and the work is lost.

In the interwar years, independent Danzig sat at the top of the Polish Corridor, a strip of land which was designed to give the resurrected Polish state access to the sea but fatally cut off German East Prussia from the rump of the shrunken Reich to the west. In the centre of the city there was a Polish Post Office, the German attack on which on 1 September 1939 is depicted so memorably in *The Tin Drum*. A company of Polish soldiers was stationed in the port on the Westerplatte, but the city's population was overwhelmingly German. Through the 1920s they were anxious, fearful and demoralized by defeat, but no more so than Germans elsewhere. The electoral fortunes of the local NSDAP were more or less the same as in the rest of the Weimar Republic, except that at the last free elections in May 1933 the party achieved an absolute majority of votes, which is more than it ever managed in Germany. German Danzig was by now showing its true colours. Hitler wanted the city 'back home in the Reich' and he made his move on the first

Günter Grass (front row centre) at cousin Helga's birthday party, 1930.

day of what became the Second World War. When he screamed in his famous radio broadcast that 'since 5.45 this morning we have been firing back', in response to alleged Polish aggression, it was the German battleship *Schleswig-Holstein* opening fire on the Westerplatte which he had in mind. The eleven-year-old Günter Grass heard the canonade. He begins his autobiography *Peeling the Onion* with an account of this day, which, he said, marked the end of his childhood.

Grass's mother Helene (née Knoff) was a Catholic Cassubian. Speaking a West Slav dialect peppered with German vocabulary and sandwiched between the Poles and the Germans, who were both inclined to look down on them, Cassubians have historically asserted a distinct folkloric identity. Helene Knoff moved from country to city to marry her German Protestant husband, following a classic pattern of local migration which entailed crossing linguistic and cultural boundaries and would often be reproduced in her son's fiction. The marital constellation is repeated in *The Tin Drum*, where to make matters more complicated, Oskar is unsure whether his biological father is his mother's husband, the practical German shopkeeper Alfred Matzerath, or his mother's cousin and lover, the dreamy Cassubian who works in the Polish Post Office, Jan Bronski. Some of Helene's family identified more with Poland than Germany. While her brothers, as subjects of the Kaiser, fought for Germany in the First World War, a cousin, Frantizek Krause, was shot by the Germans in 1939, just like Bronski in Grass's first novel. The fault-line which Hitler exploited in order to start the Second World War thus ran right through the extended Grass family. Looking back, he became aware that he and his relatives dutifully averted their gaze from the Nazis' victims among their own ranks, as well as from teachers who suddenly disappeared and the Jehovah's Witness who refused to hold a rifle in military training. 'It was not spoken about' (x:454), he remembers in *Peeling the Onion*, as so many painful topics were passed over in silence both during and after the war. As millions of Germans behaved in similar ways across the Reich, Grass came to realize after 1945 that his family history was an object

Grass with his parents and sister, Waltraud, 1932.

lesson in catastrophic dysfunction. But on his first return visit to Gdańsk in May 1958 he discovered Krause's name on a plaque commemorating the heroic defenders of the Polish Post Office. He also found out that the official version of the siege, according to which there were no Polish survivors, was not true. This taught him a lesson about history he would never forget and he duly corrected the official record in a work of fiction.

Grass often invokes binary oppositions in his political contributions, such as Nazi and Communist, NATO and the Warsaw Pact, or, in his fiction, the Apollonian and Dionysiac (*The Tin Drum*), Jew and gentile (*Dog Years*), male and female (*The Flounder*), or Stasi officer and dissident (*Too Far Afield*), only to subvert them once he discovers their similarity and sets off in search of a middle way. 'This house has two entrances', he writes in an early poem, 'I use the third' (1:137). Danzig had a significant Jewish population, whose roots reached back centuries, but it was the Polish/German split which shaped Grass's outlook, made all the more complicated because the Cassubians stood somewhere in between, offering the original 'third way' between two mutually exclusive alternatives. Danzig was undoubtedly a special place to grow up, rich in historical and artistic stimuli, situated at numerous cultural and geographical crossroads. Its modern history is brutal and tragic.

As a child Grass was a server at mass, like Pilenz in *Cat and Mouse* who was motivated to witness his friend Mahlke's frenetic worship. There is a strong Catholic dimension in much of Grass's fiction which circles around questions of guilt in a fallen world. Central chapters in *The Tin Drum* have titles like 'No Miracle',[2] 'Good Friday Fare', 'Faith, Hope, Charity' and 'Madonna 49', while Oskar takes part in a black mass and gives himself up for arrest with the statement 'I am Jesus.' The novel is steeped in Christian imagery and language, to the extent that one distinguished critic has recently identified traces of the biblical four layers of meaning.[3]

The Bible is a source of inspiration in other novels. Volker Neuhaus, an ordained Protestant pastor as well as Grass's first biographer and editor of the first complete edition of his writings, has conducted a church service using imagery and texts from Grass's oeuvre, mainly the novel of the apocalypse, *The Rat*. The culmination of millennia of false hopes in *The Flounder* is a mock crucifixion and the title of *Too Far Afield* is taken from the Bible.[4] Religion only begins to play a lesser role in the works of his last two decades. On political matters, however, the Church always got it wrong, according to Grass, not voicing a protest against Nazi persecution or coming to the aid of the victims and not facing up to the crimes of Nazism once they were over. He sometimes places Catholicism alongside communism and Nazism as an example of a totalizing set of beliefs which he rejects. He formally resigned from the Church in 1974 in protest against its opposition to abortion reform, explaining shortly afterwards that Catholicism fascinated him like a 'ginger-haired girl', on account of the remnants of paganism it incorporated.[5]

Notwithstanding the looming world war and the growing persecution of minorities within his midst, Grass's childhood does not seem to have been especially eventful. The family was poor, all sleeping in the same room above the parents' *kolonialwarengeschäft*, a kind of grocers-cum-delicatessen, selling mainly imported foodstuffs. The enforced proximity meant that the children were aware of their parents' sex life, as Grass nearly always recalled when he looked back on his past. In *Peeling the Onion* he added that, once he reached adolescence and was no longer in any doubt what the noises meant, he wanted to defend his mother against what he took to be his father's aggression. In *From the Diary of a Snail*, he had already admitted that at the age of fifteen 'I wanted to murder my father . . . with a Hitler Youth dagger' (v:358), adding that he was surely no different in this respect from any other fifteen-year-old. He also revealed in *Peeling the Onion* that, along with many other children, he was the object of a predatory priest's sexual attentions, an episode which is alluded to in *Cat and Mouse*, but he makes no attempt to elaborate on the memory. What does his regular exposure to a primal scene tell us about the artist that he grew to be? Certainly, he absorbed experiences from an early age which he later turned into art. But he is also challenging readers to interpret the shocking disclosure, at the same time as letting them realize that such an early loss of innocence was nothing unusual in the milieu in which he grew up. In *The Flounder*, the sleeping arrangements in Lena Stubbe's late nineteenth-century working-class family are identical, except that she has three daughters and is indeed regularly the victim of domestic violence. Grass is making a point here about psychoanalysis: Freud's patients were well-to-do and psychoanalysis articulates a set of myths based on bourgeois assumptions of family relations. He recognized that he had a complex about his mother and that his writing in part sprang from it, often joking that he refused any form of analysis because he wanted to be the only person earning money from it: 'The words carved on my gravestone will be: "Here lies —— with his untreated mother complex."'[6]

Grass with his mother and sister, 1934.

When it comes to sexuality Grass deploys vocabulary and imagery as explicit as the censored passages in *Lady Chatterley's Lover* or *Ulysses,* and for a while his novels were treated as equally scandalous. Sex is rarely a private affair in *The Tin Drum*. Little escapes the attention of the eternal three-year-old Oskar, who hides in wardrobes and under tables and witnesses both his parents having sex, though not with each other. *Cat and Mouse* taunts prudish readers with its depiction of a masturbation contest between teenage boys. By the 1970s, however, Grass's sexual imagination began to look one-sidedly male. In *From the Diary of a Snail*, Lisbeth Stomma is cured of her melancholia by the application of the eponymous molluscs to ever more intimate parts of her anatomy, which eventually results in sexual release. The climax of *The Flounder* entails a trio of lesbians who pass round a strap-on dildo to rape their friend as she sleeps.

His parents' marriage does not appear to have been unhappy (there was no adultery as in *The Tin Drum*), but Grass makes mother and father into another of his binary oppositions. Like Alfred Matzerath, who tells baby Oskar that he can one day take over the family business while his mother promises him a drum, Wilhelm comes out as unimaginative and uninspiring. And, of course, he joined the NSDAP: 'My father was the typical opportunistic fellow traveller,' Grass recalled in the mid-1980s. 'He joined the party in 1936. I asked him about it years after the war and he said he was more or less obliged to because the competition had joined but he also had a sense of living in historic times and he just wanted to be part of it.'[7] Recounting the story of a classmate whose father ended up in a penal battalion for listening to the BBC, then succeeded in deserting to the Red Army before playing a pioneering role in the administration of the early GDR, he remarks wistfully in *Peeling the Onion* that it is useless for him to wish that his father had been like that.

In contrast, his mother fostered her son's love of literature. She called him Peer Gynt because he would invent stories for her and she was his first and possibly most significant audience, but she never held a book in her hands with her son's name on the cover, which clearly caused him pain even into old age. His mother died more than two years before he published his first volume of poems, *The Advantages of the Wind Chickens*.[8]

Grass's comments on his parents are probably coloured by his father surviving his mother by 25 years. While he opposed his son's decision to become an artist, once the son was successful the father assured him that he had always believed in his talent, which clearly rankled. The world-famous author is moreover convinced that Wilhelm Grass appreciated the professional success of his younger sister Waltraud, who became a midwife and trade union official, more than his own rather abstract renown.[9] This rankled, too, but the lack of appreciation cut both ways. When Volker Neuhaus showed him the proofs of his first biography, Grass made only one correction, saying that his father was not a caretaker after the war in West Germany, but only an 'assistant caretaker'. In 1978 Grass told his publisher Eduard Reifferscheid that he wished his father had the same energy at eighty, but that he was already 'a broken man' in 1945 when he lost his modest livelihood: 'when my mother died in 1954, all he could do was get older and older and become ever more decrepit.'[10] This pity of defeated fathers, whether sympathetic or not, is said to be typical of the generation which took to the streets to protest against the Vietnam War. Grass argued with them when the barricades went up in 1968 but his heart seems to have beaten on their side in this respect – and given the turn his politics took in the 1980s perhaps some other respects too.

Helene was not only from the side of the family which fought the Nazis. She herself was repeatedly raped by Soviet soldiers in March 1945, offering herself to them in order to protect the fourteen-year-old Waltraud. More than a million German women are estimated to have suffered the same fate at the hands of Red Army soldiers. Grass did not mention publicly that his mother was one of them until 1979, when he chose to do so in an interview with a French writer.[11] It was another of those things which was not spoken about. *Der Spiegel*, which published a translated digest of the book-length interview, ignored the information. Grass did not draw attention to it again until 2002 with the publication of *Crabwalk*, which depicts the suffering of German civilians in 1945.

By 1979 Grass had depicted military rape twice in his fiction, briefly and half-facetiously in *The Tin Drum*, as if he was distancing himself from the topic through Oskar's black humour, and as the crescendo to centuries of male violence in *The Flounder*.[12] In *Too Far Afield*, Fonty's French mistress is tarred and feathered by vengeful compatriots after the German retreat in 1944. Fonty's reconciliation with his rediscovered French granddaughter Madeleine is the basis for the only truly happy ending in Grass's entire fiction. While Helene died of cancer, her son links her early death to her experience of rape, which aged her prematurely. He dedicated *The Flounder* to 'Helene Grass', which is both his mother's name and that of his second daughter, who was born while he was writing the novel.

Helene was the reader in the family and it was because of her that her son received a literary education, one restricted by her limited means, taste and background but a literary education nonetheless. Oskar Matzerath mentions that his mother would swoon over a volume called *Rasputin and Women*[13] and refers frequently to the nationalist historical romance set among the Vizigoths, *The Battle for Rome* by Felix Dahn, first published in 1864, as well as Gustav Freytag's 1855 epic of middle-class German virtue beset by scheming Jews and inadequate Poles, *Debit and Credit*. Helene Grass owned a broader range of romances and classics. Grass mentions Dostoyevsky (*Demons*), Raabe (*The Hunger Pastor* and *The Chronicle of Sparrow Street*), Schiller (*Collected Poems*), Theodor Storm (*The Rider on the White Horse*) and a *Bildungsroman* by Gottfried Keller, *Green Heinrich*, as well as the contemporary best-seller about life on the dole in the dying days of the Weimar Republic, Hans Fallada's *Little Man, What Now?* He devoured books wherever he came across them, developing an ability to shut himself off in his own mental world. Many of these early reading experiences stayed with him. A paternal uncle owned a copy of Erich Maria Remarque's *All Quiet on the Western Front*, probably not knowing that it was banned. In the mid-1960s Grass paid a visit to the elderly Remarque, living by this stage at Lake Maggiore in Switzerland. In the five chapters from 1914 to 1918 in *My Century* he imagines how a young Swiss scholar arranges a meeting between Remarque and his ideological counterpart Ernst Jünger, whose *Storms of Steel* conveyed a diametrically opposite impression of the war in the trenches.

Grass's early fiction is a reckoning with the nationalist fiction he read in his youth. *Dog Years* retells the friendship of the Jew and the Ayran, Eddi Amsel and Walter Matern, by reversing the relationships between Hans Unwirsch and Moses Freudenstein in *The Hunger Pastor* by Wilhelm Raabe. These novels were as influential in Germany as classics by such as Stendhal, Manzoni and Dickens in other European countries, but the difference is that their pronounced nationalist tendency made them unreadable after 1945.[14] By showing how his characters consumed such literary fare, Grass probes the *zivilisationsbruch* (caesura in civilization) which Nazism constituted and which is as evident in such everyday culture as in high politics.

Helene Grass's connections with literature were greater than her reading tastes, however. By her early twenties she was one of only two survivors from a family of five siblings. Her father was killed in 1915 at the battle of Tannenberg. Two of her brothers perished later in the First World War and a third shortly after it had ended, either in the epidemic of Spanish flu, according to *Peeling the Onion*, or of a sexually transmitted disease, according to an earlier account in *My Century*. None was older than 23. 'She talked to me all the time about her brothers'. 'Maybe she looked in me for what she had lost in them.'[15] In *Peeling the Onion*, he makes himself into his uncles' artistic heir since each had displayed a talent which their nephew, who came through the Second World War only by chance, would develop on their behalf: poetry, art and cooking.

Helene's own mother then seems to have died of grief, leaving Helene to care for a younger sister. Should we recognize Grass's maternal grandmother as Niobe, who turned to stone in mourning for her dead children, after whom Grass names a key pre-war chapter in *The Tin Drum*? Or as Oskar's mother Agnes, who gorges herself to death on fish after a terror-inducing vision of eels feeding off the head of a dead horse which is hauled out of the sea on Good Friday? When Oskar's friend Herbert Truczinski impales himself on the bewitched ship's figurehead, christened Niobe by the Danzigers, he succumbs to an eroticized death drive with a maternal symbol petrified with grief. Helene's personality must have been marked by the horrific conflicts which her son would place at the heart of his life's work.

In 1968 Grass published a slim volume of short prose entitled *Geschichten* (Stories) under the name Artur Knoff, a photograph of whom apparently graced the cover, moustachioed like Grass but thinner and younger-looking and in an awkward but nevertheless gracefully held pose astride a chair. 'Artur Knoff' is in fact the ballerina Anna Grass, got up in male drag. The little book attracted some positive notices but nobody realized it was a prank until the beans were spilt twenty years later by a confidant, Grass's editor, Klaus Roehler. Grass expressed himself astonished to a fellow conspirator that their deception on the nation's book reviewers should have succeeded so easily.[16] The prose fantasies now take their place in Grass's experimental oeuvre, belonging closer to his poetry than his epic narratives, but what is most remarkable about the hoax is his choice of pseudonym and of his wife Anna to play the part of the long deceased Artur Knoff. Presenting *Geschichten* in this way was more than an act of posthumous restitution to a dead uncle. After all, Grass could have disguised himself or asked a male friend. Could it be that through his wife impersonating his mother's brother, he is acknowledging that his mother also writes through him? A resurrected Helene Grass presides over the collection of 100 stories in *My Century*, narrating the very last one, '1999', as she looks forward to her 103rd birthday. She is now living in an old people's home, which her son has chosen for her and where he visits her with his children and grandchildren. He still tells her stories, as he did when he was a child, though she has not approved always of his choice of subject-matter. The account of her death from cancer in *Peeling the Onion* and his failure to pay her due attention because he was too busy with his own affairs (his studies, his fiancée, his budding artistic and literary career) is among the most moving and rhythmically powerful passages he ever wrote. He married Anna three months after his mother's death.

Grass left school at fifteen to man an anti-aircraft battery on the coast at Kaisershafen with other boys of his age. Lessons were intermittent from now on; in *Dog Years*, Sergeant Walter Matern is a military instructor at the same base, which is also attended by Harry Liebenau, who narrates the middle 'Love Letters' section of Grass's second novel. Grass had already twice been expelled from school for misdemeanours, moving from a Gymnasium (the Conradinum in Langfuhr) to the technical upper school (*oberrealschule*) of St Peter and St Paul and from there to the Sankt Johann Gymnasium in the historic centre of the city. This forced move would be of great benefit to his fiction because he got to know the narrow streets, the wharves and waterways, the distinct districts, and above all the ecclesiastical buildings of old Danzig.[17] He suffered the supposed ignominy of repeating a year of schooling (*sitzenbleiben*) because of low marks. While he got As in German and drawing and Bs in history and geography, he was failing in chemistry, Latin and English and it looked likely he would not pass the *Abitur* when the time came. His parents made sacrifices to pay school 'entrance fees' for their talented son but could not help him with his homework or send him to a tutor, as other parents did.[18] His experience of selective schools made him into a lifelong advocate of comprehensive education.

He recalls a number of staff in these all-male institutions and often remarked on how teachers, often based on those he knew, featured in his fiction. In *The Tin Drum* and *Cat and Mouse* there are some memorably narrow-minded or ineffectual teachers, such as Fräulein Spollenhauer, who tries to remove Oskar's drum on his first and only day at school, or the headmaster Klose, who refuses to allow Mahlke to address the school about his experiences at the front; but in *Dog Years* Papa Brunies behaves with understated heroism. Grass gives teachers a central role in *Local Anaesthetic* (Eberhard Starusch), *From the Diary of a Snail* (Hermann Ott) and *Headbirths* (Harm and Dörte Peters). At least two of his own teachers made a positive impression, at least retrospectively. Dr Stachnik, who was obsessed with the fourteenth-century mystic Dorothea von Montau, as Grass records in *The Flounder*, was the chairman of the pre-war Catholic Centre Party (forerunner of the post-war Christian Democrats) and saw the inside of Stutthof concentration camp for his failure to toe the line. Another was a rather conservative teacher of history who peppered his explanations of events with the words 'doubt' and 'doubtful' (like Hermann Ott, whose nickname is Doubt) and once referred to the German people as 'lemmings' (XII:535). One day he disappeared after some sixth-formers, so it was said, reported him, as somebody also reported Papa Brunies, who dies in Stutthof in November 1943. The history teacher was never seen again but everyone knew that he too was in Stutthof. In *Peeling the Onion*, as the military is disintegrating and he is running away in the midst of defeat, Grass comes to respect the advice of a series of slightly older non-commissioned officers. After the war, his attitude to mentor figures undergoes a sea change, as he begins positively to seek them out, as writers *in spe* often do. Grass also always paid tribute to the staff at the Art Academies in

Düsseldorf and Berlin, for instance, such as Sepp Mages, Otto Pankok and Gabriel Ludwig Schreiber, to name but three who are portrayed in his fiction. *Peeling the Onion* is 'Dedicated to everybody I learnt from'.

German *gymnasien* were not usually welcoming institutions. That is certainly the impression gained from reading fictional accounts of school by Thomas and Heinrich Mann (*Buddenbrooks* and *Professor Unrat*), Hermann Hesse (*Beneath the Wheel*) and Frank Wedekind (*Spring Awakening*). Compared with these nightmarish scenarios of sadism, repression and rote learning written or set in the late nineteenth century, Grass got off lightly, which, he surmised, is probably because most of the regular teachers had been called up and wartime schooling was pretty chaotic. All the same he does not believe that he learned much and he was obliged to teach himself what he later came to value about his education, and he never went back to school to complete his *abitur*. In the subjects which were important to him – literature, history, theology and philosophy – he was an autodidact. Reflecting in 1980 on the problems his teenage children faced in school, he confided to his friend, the British novelist Eva Figes, that he sometimes regarded it as a piece of good fortune that he stopped at fifteen: 'I have had to teach myself everything.'[19]

One of the biggest planks in the public platform which Grass constructed for himself from the mid-1960s, when he began to make contributions to politics and debate, was his year of birth. It made him old enough to have experienced Nazism at first hand but too young to have made compromises with the regime. He and colleagues such as Hans Magnus Enzensberger (b. 1929), Peter Rühmkorf (1929–2008) and Martin Walser (b. 1927) possessed, in Sigrid Weigel's phrase, 'knowledge without guilt'.[20] 'You're right,' Grass tells his children in *From the Diary of a Snail* when they ask him what they should think of the past, 'you are innocent. I too, born just about late enough, count as not incriminated' (v:295). The year 1927 was a 'white year', which largely explains why members of his age group enjoyed disproportionate opportunities and prestige in the Federal Republic. In the wake of Grass's belated admission that he was called up to the ss rather than the Wehrmacht, they faced a belated reckoning.[21] Yet the impersonal 'count as' and the negative 'not incriminated' (in German *unbelastet*) in the passage quoted show his uncertainty about his real status. In March 1967 he told an audience in Israel:

> As a fourteen-year-old I was in the Hitler Youth; at sixteen I became a soldier and at seventeen I was an American prisoner of war . . . My year of birth says: I was too young to have been a Nazi but old enough to have been shaped by a system which between 1933 and 1945 made the world gasp, first in astonishment then in horror.[22]

After three obligatory months of 'labour service' in the early summer of 1944 which followed on from the stint at the anti-aircraft battery, Grass awaited his inevitable call-up, which arrived a few weeks before his seventeenth birthday. This was a classic wartime career for an adolescent in Grass's year cohort and was followed by male contemporaries as diverse in other respects as Walser (fellow novelist), Hans-Dietrich Genscher (foreign minister, 1974–92), and Joseph Ratzinger (Pope Benedict XVI, 2005–13), all of whom were born in 1927. The male heroes in Grass's fiction follow very similar paths: Mahlke in *Cat and Mouse*, Liebenau in *Dog Years* and Alexander Reschke in *The Call of the Toad* all joined the 'military' at seventeen, though whether this was the regular Wehrmacht or the Waffen-ss Grass does not spell out. Often it mattered little by the last year of the war as the distinctions had become blurred. When talking about himself he preferred neutral phrases such as 'I was called up', 'I became a tank-gunner' or 'I joined the military.' By and large, critics summarizing his life followed suit, almost certainly without realizing what they were doing, but he did not correct anyone who said Wehrmacht, as Neuhaus did in the first edition of his biography.[23] Grass never made a secret of his unquestioning 'faith' in the Nazi creed, which is shared by most of his major novel characters, or of the fact that, had he been three or four years older, it is likely that he would have become involved in atrocities: 'I cannot guarantee that I would have had sufficient defence mechanisms. I don't think so, I was not trained, not equipped that way.'[24] Seventeen is the key age for many male characters in his fiction, from Philip Scherbaum in *Local Anaesthetic* to Konrad Pokriefke in *Crabwalk*. It is synonymous with faith in an ideology which promises salvation, offers answers to all life's questions, and divides people up into clear categories. In his public pronouncements Grass sketched out his biographical progress in order to stress its typicality and the ordinariness of the life-changing episode which followed. But it was not until *Peeling the Onion* that he revealed that, after an unsuccessful application to become a submariner, he was chosen for the ss. Until this admission, which made headlines around the world, he expected his listeners to assume that he joined the regular army (the Wehrmacht), but he never explicitly said that he did. Sometimes he hinted differently, such as in an alternative biography in *Headbirths* when he admits that the Danzig ss-*Heimwehr* (Home Defence Force) could have counted on him had he turned seventeen at the beginning rather than at the end of the war.[25] When he expanded on his military training, the mortar attack which killed half his company and his capture by the Americans, the account is the same as that narrated in *Peeling the Onion*, where he only adds more incidental and often novelistic detail.

Grass warned Michael Jürgs not to call his literary characters alter egos,[26] but they do act out parallel careers to him: Oskar is three years older, stopping his growth, so as to remain permanently in the shape of a child, on his third birthday in 1927, but Pilenz and Mahlke (*Cat and Mouse*); Liebenau, Tulla and Jenny Brunies (*Dog Years*); Starusch (*Local Anaesthetic*) and both Reschke and the anonymous narrator in *The Call of the Toad* are direct contemporaries. The males pass through the same formative sequence of Hitler Youth, anti-aircraft gunner, labour service and military call-up – Starusch, who does not mention the military, ends up in Grass's POW camp at Bad Aibling, while Mahlke, who goes straight from labour service to the army, and Liebenau both wanted to join the crew of a submarine but ended up in a tank, just like Grass. Amsel and Matern, on the other hand, are exactly a decade older, which gives them time to experience the Nazi years as young adults. Grass went over the same autobiographical ground compulsively in his fiction before finally writing his own account in the semi-fictional autobiography *Peeling the Onion*.

Looking back in 2006 Grass is sure that in 1944 he would have been proud to have been chosen for the Waffen-SS. As an elite component of the Nazi war machine they were reputed to take only the best, but he does not explain why he misled by omission for the previous forty or more years. After his company scattered in March 1945 in the wake of an attack and he roamed fearfully through woodland, he learnt that he must get rid of the insignia and any bits of uniform which would identify him as an SS soldier. The reason was simple: the Red Army took the Wehrmacht prisoner while they executed the SS on the spot. Perhaps this is when he learnt to keep quiet. But in the 1960s, when he presented his biography as a moral lesson to the nation, the detail of SS membership could have made it all the more convincing. His attacks on the war heroes who were proud of their *Ritterkreuz* (Knight's Cross) or on revanchists from the lost territories, not to mention his tirades against ex-NSDAP member Kurt Georg Kiesinger, CDU chancellor from 1966 to 1969, would have had a different but surely more compelling timbre too.

The end of the war found the seventeen-year-old tank-gunner Günter Grass in a military hospital in the old Sudetenland spa town of Marienbad. He had been wounded near Cottbus to the south of Berlin and understood the news of the unconditional surrender to be a defeat rather than a liberation, assuming vaguely, insofar as he was thinking about it at all, that the fighting would soon start up again. Grass was lucky to be taken prisoner by the Americans rather than the Soviets, who soon took over Marienbad once it reverted to Czechoslovakia and its German population was expelled, like that of Danzig. Along with other POWs he was taken to Dachau in the summer of 1945 but was sure that the evidence of mass murder was faked. Once released from his POW camp, however, in the autumn of 1946, he listened to broadcasts of the Nuremberg Trials and slowly came to accept their horrific truth and to place it in the context of his own experience. The rupture signalled by 1945 and the realization that he had been complicit in the greatest acts of barbarism which the world had ever seen gradually overwhelmed his sense of himself. Grass learned to live in a faithless world, which is reflected in his inversion of Catholic metaphysics, joy in earthly pleasures, interest in absurdist literature and French Existentialism and, subsequently, his politics. Grass's re-invention of himself must count as one of the most stunning long-term success stories of the Allies' post-war Re-education Programme.

On release he owned nothing except the clothes he was wearing and had no idea where the rest of his family might be. Grass may not have been in sympathy with the spirit of the economic miracle which saw the bombed-out cities quickly rebuilt, but he worked as determinedly to achieve success and recognition in his field as any of the other washed-up expellees, to whom the success of the new republic can in no small measure be attributed. Grass worked first in the fields and then in a potash mine near Hildesheim in Lower Saxony. Here, nearly a kilometre underground, he learnt a political lesson which stayed with him all his life. Listening to political discussions between old Nazis, communists and social democrats, he noticed how a pattern established during the 1920s was repeating itself: Left and Right ganged up on the moderates in the middle, an alliance which proved fatal in the days of Weimar. When he found his family again in December 1946 they were penniless refugees lodging in an outhouse owned by a grudging farmer. In the last chapter of *My Century*, he imagines his mother remembering:

> we got shoved out, to the Soviet Zone first, but then we fled to the West, where some Rhineland peasants put us in the ice-cold room they used for storing fodder, and wouldn't leave us in peace with their 'Why don't you go back to where you came from!' And they were as Catholic as me . . . (IX:331)

They were now a family of *heimatvertriebene* (expellees). Salman Rushdie, another imitator who became a friend, explained that Grass in fact migrated twice, across time from the Third Reich to the freedom of the post-war republic, as well as westwards from Danzig.[27] He became a different person, looking back on his young self as an alien entity.

Grass qualified as a monumental mason, specializing in head-stones, before enrolling to study sculpture, first in Düsseldorf, then West Berlin. In Düsseldorf he shared a dormitory in a *caritasheim* (communal digs for young men funded by the Catholic Church) and played the washboard in a jazz band. He began to use his summers to discover the world through travel, to Italy in 1951 in the footsteps of Dürer, Goethe and Mann. The Italian experiences were foundational:

> I lived: that is, I took in everything, could never get enough, and hard as I tried, I could do nothing to reduce the splendours before me. I stood thunderstruck before gesticulating marble,

entranced before hand-size Etruscan bronzes. I looked up Vasari
in Florence and Arezzo . . .

I drew whatever landscape, street or square placed before
my eyes, excreting verse as usual, evoking the stagnant heat
of the midday calm or a fountain in a shady park. (x:534)

He hitch-hiked to France the following summer, living cheaply,
sketching and writing poetry all the while.

In April 1954, three months after the death of his mother, he
married the daughter of a highly respectable Swiss German family,
the dance student Anna Schwarz. Like any young newly-wed, Grass
wanted to pay his own way in life but from this point he knew that
he did not need to worry about money. For the first time in his life
he no longer needed to share a bedroom either, except with his
new wife. His in-laws owned a holiday house in Brittany, which
they placed at the young couple's disposal, and in December 1956
they bought them a small ground-floor flat in the Avenue d'Italie
in Paris, where Grass would write *The Tin Drum*. After Anna gave
birth to twins in September 1957 her parents even paid for a live-in
nanny. Grass likes to recall the Parisian period as one of bohemian
poverty but he in fact enjoyed more than basic bourgeois comforts.
The marriage was enriching in other respects. The Swiss are the
most experienced democrats in Europe and Anna's parents had
no Nazi skeletons in their cupboard. They also had a house full
of books.

One of the secrets of Grass's immense productivity over six full
decades is that he learnt to alternate periods of intense concentration
with family, travel or work in the art studio. He valued rural retreats,
owning a chalet in the Swiss village of Gordevio in the 1960s,
splitting his time between Berlin and Wewelsfleth in Schleswig-
Holstein the following decade and renting a cottage on the Baltic
island of Møn after marriage to Ute while also owning an apartment
on the Algarve. At each location he kitted out a studio where he could

Grass with Anna née Schwarz on their wedding day, 1954.

Grass with Anna and her parents on the couple's wedding day, 1954.

On holiday in Gordevio, 1969/70.

work in clay, copper or bronze and a study with a waist-high writing desk at which he stood upright as he wrote or typed. The change of scenery helped him with his work. It is a routine which he learnt right at the beginning of his career, when he alternated between Ticino in Switzerland, which was Anna's family home, the couple's flat in Paris and the Schwarz family cottage in Brittany.

Anna Schwarz was a trainee ballerina and the marriage was an artistic partnership. Her impact was greatest on *Dog Years* but dance also features in the tragic sequence on a Normandy beach in *The Tin Drum*. Grass wrote ballets for a while and was commissioned by Walter Höllerer to write an essay on the theory of composition and performance, which he entitled 'The Ballerina'. He and Anna moved to Paris because she wanted to dance under the renowned 'Madame Nora' (Nora Kiss). Anna also played the more traditional female role of muse and helpmeet, as well as mother of the artist's children; in return he dedicated *The Tin Drum* to her. In *My Century* '1959' is her chapter. It takes the form of a single swirling sentence which recounts how they danced together at the Frankfurt Book Fair as *The Tin Drum* was taking the literary world by storm. Dance was Anna's art form, though yet another which Grass mastered with apparent effortlessness and would continue to practise long after their marriage was over, with gusto and high seriousness judging by the photographs he published in his *Studio Reports*. One of his last book of poems is called *Last Dances*.

As Grass turned thirty in October 1957, the age at which Oskar is released from his psychiatric hospital at the end of *The Tin Drum*, the need to earn a decent living was becoming more acute. His first volume of 'poems and drawings' was published in 1956 with his own cover design, setting a pattern which he repeated with

Grass in the courtyard of Avenue d'Italie, Paris; Anna at the window, *c.* 1956.

every subsequent publication for the next six decades, whatever its genre. Sales were reasonable for a first volume of poems (in the low hundreds). Galleries also showed themselves ready to exhibit his art (Stuttgart, 1955; Berlin, 1957) and his plays and ballets were getting performances (*Flood* in 1957; *Uncle, Uncle* in 1958; and the ballet *Material Scraps* in 1957). He was receiving paid invitations to read poems on regional radio and 'reading poetry for cash' gave him a good feeling. He was signed up by the young theatrical agent and publisher Maria Sommer, who became a lifelong friend and manager of the stage and screen rights to all his works. His poems are about art and tactile experience; they are hard-edged and unsentimental, characterized by word-play, humour and literary inventiveness, often giving sound and image primacy over sense. They are perhaps best appreciated in live performance, which Grass perfected from this time. His plays depict rather abstract scenarios and engage more directly with ideas. They were not a route to fame and fortune, however.

He was reading all the time. His art teacher Ludwig Gabriel Schrieber recommended De Coster's *Ulenspiegel*, Paul Celan the

Walter Höllerer, Berlin, *c.* 1960.

novels of Rabelais, whose earthy Renaissance erudition influenced Grass's style from *The Tin Drum* to *The Meeting in Telgte*. He recalls too immersing himself in the modernist works of Joyce, Döblin and Dos Passos which he found on his in-laws' bookshelves. As the decade progressed he switched his attention to writing his own epic work of prose. These were no longer chance literary encounters: this was creative writing training and the syllabus was international and increasingly contemporary. Along with Hans Jakob Christoffel Grimmelshausen and the Romantic humourist Jean Paul, these writers would make up a private tradition which Grass would still be citing at the end of his life. In his last volume of poems, *Mayflies*, he imagines conversations with both Grimmelshausen and Jean Paul and invokes the memory of Rabelais.

Walter Höllerer, the editor of the literary magazine *Akzente*, rented himself an apartment in the same block in the Avenue d'Italie, apparently with no other aim than to support Grass, supplying books from Germany on request and paying commissions for his poetry magazine. The literary world which congregated around the Gruppe 47 fostered his precocious and obvious talent from May 1955, when he first read some poems, to October 1958 when he won its coveted prize for a performance of two chapters from his unpublished first novel. Grass sold his artwork at meetings and was encouraged to persevere with his novel (in particular, he recalls, by the writer Paul Schallück), all the while taking the measure of his more senior colleagues.[28] They met once or twice a year for two or three days under the chairmanship of Hans Werner Richter, each participant reading from a work in progress which was then discussed by the listeners, the author not being permitted to respond. Usually a prize was awarded and each meeting attracted more media attention than the last one. For Grass it was a way of meeting a large number of writers, poets, publishers and critics who formed part of a rising establishment in the new republic, all loosely on the left, a counter-voice to the ethos of Adenauer and the economic miracle. The writers included Alfred Andersch, Ingeborg Bachmann, Heinrich Böll and Peter Weiss. Grass enjoyed the sense of common purpose and solidarity, which he tried repeatedly to recreate after the group was wound up in 1968 – the meeting that year which was due to take place in Prague was cancelled after Soviet tanks put an end to the reformist communist government under Alexander Dubček.

Hans Werner Richter with Hans Magnus Engensberger, 1963.

Paul Schallück, 1956.

In Paris Grass lived a quiet life, though he got himself arrested in 1958 during disturbances when the ill-conceived Fourth Republic collapsed and General de Gaulle returned to the presidency. His contact with Parisians was by his own admission sporadic. He and Anna paid a call on the Polish émigré Czesław Miłosz to convey Grass's admiration for his reckoning with communism in *The Captive Mind* (1953), which next to books by Albert Camus and George Orwell was shaping his reformist political outlook.[29]

The major contemporary French reading experience of the 1950s is Camus, whose side Grass instinctively took in his argument with Sartre over the character of *littérature engagée* and the role of the committed writer. Camus' version of the Sisyphus myth remained another fixed point of reference, but it is *The Rebel*, written in response to the dual catastrophes of Nazism and Stalinism, which reads more like a forerunner to Grass's own political philosophy.[30] Camus, born in 1913, the same year as Brandt, had also had a good war. In his writings he took on the big metaphysical and political questions about values and meaning in a godless world from the perspective of European history and philosophy. Camus opposed revolution, whether from the left or the right, because he believed that revolutions increased the power of the state, as demonstrated repeatedly since 1789. In his search for a non-revolutionary way forward, Camus proposed 'rebellion'. *The Rebel* closes with some dialectical thoughts which leave their traces in *The Tin Drum* and which Grass develops more fully in *From the Diary of a Snail*:

> Moderation, born of rebellion, can only live by rebellion. It is a perpetual conflict, continually created and mastered by the intelligence. It does not triumph either in the impossible or the abyss. It finds its equilibrium through them . . . We all carry within us our places of exile, our crimes, and our ravages. But our task is not to unleash them on the world; it is to fight them in ourselves and in others.[31]

Grass's friendship of note in the Paris period is with the Jewish Rumanian German-language poet Paul Celan, a French citizen since 1948 who taught translation at the École normale supérieure. It is likely to have been Höllerer who facilitated their meeting shortly after Günter and Anna moved into the Avenue d'Italie. The 'difficult' friendship left its mark on the work of both men and endured until Grass returned in triumph to Berlin as the author of *The Tin Drum*. Their correspondence peters out in 1966, four years before Celan's suicide,[32] but Celan followed Grass's career to the end and acquired copies of just about all his books as they came out.[33] He even taught *The Tin Drum*, using the copy Grass had signed for him, in which he made his last annotation on 15 April 1970, possibly just five days before he threw himself into the Seine. He marked up Oskar's curiously confident comment at the beginning of 'Niobe' that willed human forgetfulness of wartime wrongdoing was bound to fail:

Today I know that objects are all witnesses, that nothing goes
unseen, that even wallpaper has a better memory than human
beings. It is not God in heaven who sees everything! A kitchen
chair, a coat-hanger, a half-full ashtray or the wooden image
of a woman called Niobe are enough to deliver each deed to
a witness with a memory. (III:247)

Grass was impressed by the older poet's precise knowledge of
literature, took his advice about what he should read (in addition
to Rabelais, the French Symbolists and the decadent fin-de-siècle
novelist Joris-Karl Huysmans), but was not attracted to Celan's
auratic bearing, which he associated with the pre-war cult around
Stefan George. He also showed limited understanding of Celan's
growing obsession with malicious allegations of plagiarism made
against Celan by Claire Goll, whose absurd claims that he had
copied some of her late husband's writings were for a time upheld
by a German court.

For *The Tin Drum*, Grass needed to address the Jewish experience
in Nazi Germany and he could not do so from his own memory. Was
it this consideration which motivated Höllerer to introduce the two
German-speaking Paris residents? Celan helped him with sections
of *The Tin Drum* by sharing his experiences in Nazi-occupied south-
eastern Europe.[34] They must have made grim listening: his parents
were deported to a work camp in 1942, where his mother was shot
and his father died of typhus. He was enlisted himself as a forced
labourer. Celan was a *nom de plume*, an anagram of his family name,
Ancel (Rumanian) or Antschel (German), which Grass would adapt
in *Dog Years*: Eddi Amsel, who himself has a number of aliases
(such as Brauxel or Brauchsel and Little Gold Mouth), orchestrates
the production of that multi-narrator novel, which rakes through
the same history as *The Tin Drum* for a second time. The Jewish
Sigismund Markus, who is in love with Oskar's mother and commits
suicide on the Kristallnacht, may have been inspired by Celan,[35]

as well as Mariusz Fajngold, a Treblinka survivor and the novel's second Jewish figure, who still does a roll-call of his once numerous family after he lodges with the surviving Matzeraths in liberated Danzig. Ferdinand Schmuh, the most neurotic character in *The Tin Drum*, who relieves his stress by shooting sparrows, is the third Jewish figure, associated with the Central European cities of Vienna and Budapest.[36] The three Jews appear at significant points in the novel – Schmuh towards the end of book three, Markus and Fajngold at the ends of books one and two respectively. Fajngold is linked thematically with Markus: as Agnes Matzerath turned down Markus's proposal to elope to London, so Oskar's widowed stepmother Maria rejects Fajngold's offer of marriage in 1945. Schmuh officiates at an establishment called the Onion Cellar in post-war Düsseldorf in which the repressed burghers of the newly founded republic find emotional release by crying over their onion-chopping boards. He dies in a car crash one afternoon after mistakenly shooting thirteen instead of his usual twelve sparrows.

The connection between Celan and the half-Jewish scarecrow-maker Eddi Amsel in *Dog Years* may go some way to explaining why Amsel makes his trauma into the source of his art after 1945. It still may jar with some readers that Amsel becomes a successful businessman whose artistic production makes him a captain of post-war industry: Amsel survives as an artist rather than as a Jew, however, and the point about him is that he can become whatever others believe or want him to be. Grass is here borrowing an idea first articulated by Sartre and made famous by Max Frisch in a post-Brechtian drama, *Andorra* (1961): 'Jewishness' is an ideological construction which is imposed on an individual by others. Amsel's father countered rumours that he was Jewish by taking up activities which the Jewish anti-Semite Otto Weininger declared non-Jewish in his highly influential tract, *Sex and Character*. Grass returned to the subject of the Holocaust repeatedly, with greatest emphasis in *From the Diary of a Snail*, for which he consulted the historian

Erwin Lichtenstein, and *Crabwalk*, in which he reverses the idea of an imposed Jewish identity, thus continuing a strand of narrative begun in *Dog Years*. Grass met Lichtenstein, a journalist in Danzig in the 1920s, on his first visit to Israel in 1967. He wrote *From the Diary of a Snail* in parallel with Lichtenstein's history of the Jews of Danzig under the Nazis, which was published the following year.[37] In *Crabwalk*, the seventeen-year-old Wolfgang Stremplin pretends he is Jewish in order to atone for Nazi crimes, even offering himself to be murdered by Tulla Pokriefke's neo-Nazi grandson, Konrad.

After Celan, Grass enjoyed numerous friendships and close working relationships with surviving German Jews. Some were émigrés, such as his American publisher Helen Wolff, the translator Michael Hamburger or the London-based writer Eva Figes and publisher Tom Rosenthal. He counted two of the most accomplished German-Jewish novelists as friends. Jurek Becker survived the concentration camps as a child, then emigrated with his father to Berlin because his father calculated that Germany would now be safer as it was not the Polish anti-Semites who had lost the war. Grass mentions his name quite frequently in *From Germany to Germany: Diary, 1990*. Wolfgang Hildesheimer spent the Nazi period in the UK and British-mandated Palestine before settling in Switzerland. He met Grass at the Gruppe 47 meetings in the mid-1950s and corresponded with him about *The Flounder*, which he reviewed in *Merkur*, and *The Meeting in Telgte*.

There were two other prominent Holocaust survivors, working on either side of the Atlantic, who never warmed to Grass's writing. Unease over his handling of recent Jewish history may have been a factor in both cases. One is the writer and critic Ruth Klüger, who as an academic published as Ruth K. Angress. She found the sexual politics of *The Flounder* to be regressive, as feminist theorists to this day are wont to do.[38] Then, in a seminal essay, published in English and German, she judged that *The Tin Drum* was one of a number of post-1945 German novels with a 'Jewish problem' on the grounds

Marcel Reich-Ranicki, 1963.

that Sigismund Markus was a stereotype assembled from anti-Semitic clichés.[39] Grass's other prominent Jewish critic is Marcel Reich-Ranicki, the 'literature pope' of the Federal Republic, host of the television programme *Das Literarische Quartett* from 1988 until 2001 and for up to half a century the doyen of German newspaper reviewers who wrote for the *Frankfurter Allgemeine Zeitung*, *Der Spiegel* and *Die Zeit*. Reich-Ranicki and Grass endured a fascinating professional rivalry which spanned both their long careers and included some bitter disputes, usually followed by tactical reconciliations. They both announced themselves to the literary world at the Gruppe 47 meeting in October 1958, when Grass won the prize and Reich-Ranicki, who had recently emigrated from Poland, attended for the first time. In 2006 they were found to be among the three most influential intellectual figures in Germany (Grass was in first place, Reich-Ranicki in third).[40] They died within a year and a half of each other, Reich-Ranicki in September 2013 at the age of 92.

The pair first met in May 1958 in Warsaw. The critic was not impressed by the poet as a person (and later accused him of being drunk) and did not think that his plans for a novel about a dwarf in a mental hospital recounting his past life sounded promising. On publication of *The Tin Drum*, Reich-Ranicki found plenty to criticize, though he soon afterwards realized he had made a mistake and said so in public.[41] He reviewed most other books by Grass, passing harsh judgements on *Local Anaesthetic*, *The Flounder*, *The Rat*, *The Call of the Toad*, and – infamously – *Too Far Afield*, but praising *The Meeting in Telgte* and the poems about sensual pleasures in old age contained in *Last Dances*. The criticisms he made of Grass's style and compositional technique were based on judicious close reading and never plucked from the air. The same could even be said too of much of his review of *Too Far Afield*, which became notorious for two essentially extraneous reasons: the photo-montage of Reich-Ranicki tearing up the book which *Der Spiegel* used as that week's cover, which he claimed was not his responsibility, and his subsequent performance on *Das Literarische Quartett*, which most certainly was.

As Grass was on a research mission to Warsaw in May 1958, it is a little odd that he did not ask his Polish contact about his wartime background. Had he done so, he would have discovered that Reich-Ranicki, deported to Poland by the Nazis as a schoolboy in 1938, survived most of the war in the Warsaw Ghetto. At the Gruppe 47 meeting in Großholzleute later that year Grass made up for his reticence, quizzing the new arrival in the Federal Republic with the distinctly abrupt and – given Grass's emphasis elsewhere on the artificiality of identity construction – uncharacteristic enquiry: 'What are you then actually? Polish, German or what?'[42] Reich-Ranicki would discover that not many people in the FRG would want to know about his past – the first exception was Ulrike Meinhof.[43] At Großholzleute, Reich-Ranicki decided to recount a rather 'harmless' episode about his entertaining the Polish couple who sheltered him with tales from the German classics. Grass asked if he could one day use the story and Reich-Ranicki consented. Fourteen years later, however, he was upset when Grass adapted it in *From the Diary of a Snail*: the host becomes the equivocating Cassubian, Anton Stomma, and the Jewish fugitive, the teacher Hermann Ott, 'alias Doubt', a fictional 'good German' who is sometimes taken to be Jewish because of his refusal to fall into line with the Nazi regime. In other words, Grass was appropriating Reich-Ranicki's Jewish story, while remaining in ignorance about what really happened to him because he had not asked. Stomma is an opportunist who keeps Ott as an insurance policy in case the Germans lose the war and he has to curry favour with the winners. According to Reich-Ranicki, his protectors were motivated by 'pity, kindness, humanity'.[44] *From the Diary of a Snail* is the only book by Grass which Reich-Ranicki never discussed, either in a newspaper review or elsewhere.

2

Art and Violence in the Early Fiction

In his first four prose works (three novels and one novella), published over a busy ten-year period between 1959 and 1969, Grass writes through a series of fictional male narrators-cum-authors about pre-1945 Danzig and the post-war transition to the Federal Republic. The narrative present (1952–4 in *The Tin Drum*, 1961–2 in *Cat and Mouse* and *Dog Years*, 1967 in *Local Anaesthetic*) assumes a more central role each time.

The narrator-authors are all involved in the arts in one way or another. An artistic bent can find an outlet in violence (Mahlke in *Cat Mouse*, Matern in *Dog Years*, the older Starusch in *Local Anaesthetic*) or undirected revolt (the younger Starusch and Oskar in *The Tin Drum*). More often art represents an escape from the self and the world, a form of protest which is equated with pleasure, even self-indulgence and freedom from responsibility.[1]

The narrators after *The Tin Drum* sometimes show knowledge of the other fiction, which is part of a meta-fictional strategy: Grass wants his readers to bear in mind, if they will, that they are dealing with a fictional version of the world as presented in works of narrative literature and that creating such a world in fiction is in part a reaction to traumatic experience.[2]

There are numerous crossovers in personnel, though the recurring characters lead more or less different existences each time. The four books are connected too, of course, by the location of Danzig, in particular its western suburb of Langfuhr (Polish:

Wrzeszcz), the mouth of the Vistula and the Cassubian hinterland. The continuities do not stop in *Local Anaesthetic*. Oskar gets a mention in *The Flounder* and is revived as a fully fledged character, now sixty years old with a weak prostate, in *The Rat*. *The Call of the Toad* centres on two Danzig contemporaries, now in their mid-sixties, at the time of the collapse of communism in Eastern Europe. Finally, in *Peeling the Onion* Grass presents his younger self in the same historical context, pre-war, war and post-war, and in relation to the same themes of shame, loss, slips of memory and artistic compulsion.

Grass is linguistically playful and often funny, unabashed in his depiction of sex, religion and violence, and above all not shy to make connections between the very ordinary lives of his respectable characters and the crimes which were committed in their midst, often with their connivance and support, even active participation. In particular in *The Tin Drum* and *Cat and Mouse*, which have remained the most popular, he delighted or appalled readers, depending on their age, taste and background. The rest of this chapter assesses how content (the actions of individuals under Nazism and in its aftermath) is expressed through form (literary genre, language) and how Grass shows how the recent past continues to disfigure the present, from which vantage point each of the ambiguous tales is reconstructed.

The Tin Drum

Oskar Matzerath's reminiscences stretch from his maternal grandparents' meeting on a Cassubian potato field in October 1899 through to his arrest for murder in 1952 and release from a psychiatric unit two years later. The reader is left in no doubt that the author of this story has been locked up because he is judged to be out of his mind and dangerous: he sits on a bed with metal railings around it and is under regular observation. This is a traditional modernist setting for a first-person confessional narrator – Dostoyevsky's anonymous first-person narrator in *Notes from Underground* (1864) could count as the prototype; the genre had been recently revived in German with *Stiller* (1954) by Max Frisch, whom Grass met in Zurich through his in-laws as he was writing *The Tin Drum*.[3]

Grass took his inspiration from an eclectic variety of other sources, including Grimmelshausen and the Grimms, J. D. Salinger and Camus, Mann and Kafka, Rabelais, Tolstoy, Sterne, Melville and Joyce. His first novel is in part a parody of Germany's greatest contribution to the novel genre, the *Bildungsroman* or novel of education, whose greatest exponent was Goethe in *Wilhelm Meister*.[4] In place of the harmonization of individual and collective interests which occurs when the hero assumes a satisfying role in society at the conclusion to such a novel, the episodes in his life all falling retrospectively into a meaningful pattern which pointed all along to such an outcome, *The Tin Drum* depicts no coherence to lived experience. For Oskar, returning to the active social world, as he is obliged to do once found innocent of murder, is a horrific prospect because he must face 'the black cook' of nursery-rhyme lore, who symbolizes a malign force which animates the world. There is an equally great difference to the seventeenth-century picaresque. Grimmelshausen's Simplicissimus confesses his life story from a desert island, having repented his sins and become ready to see the world's random cruelty as an inverse reflection of eternity. Grass's Oskar can find neither transcendence nor meaning.

The Tin Drum is essentially episodic, many of the chapters narrating neatly self-contained sequences, such as Oskar's love affair with public performances, which culminate in his hilarious subversion of a Nazi rally (which is rendered so memorably in Schlöndorff's film), the fateful family outing to the seaside in 'Good Friday Fare', or the journey to the West in a crowded goods wagon

Anna Bronski (Tina Engel) offers shelter under her four skirts to her fugitive husband Josef Koljaiczek on the potato field in the heart of Cassubia near Danzig, in Volker Schlöndorff's film *The Tin Drum* (1979).

at the end of the war. Passages of realist narration give way to associative prose poems or fantastic incidents, such as Oskar's cracking of the glass casings in the doctor's surgery with his ear-piercing scream or his dream vision of the infernal children's merry-go-round which is inspired by the news that thousands of children have been drowned fleeing from the Soviets in the winter of 1945. The chapters have titles, which novel chapters have tended not to have since the eighteenth century (Jean Paul and Grimmelshausen use them). These are usually a name ('Niobe', 'Maria', 'Klepp'), a noun or noun phrase ('The Photograph Album', 'The Time Table', 'The Rostrum', 'The House of Cards', 'Fizz Powder' or 'The Ring Finger'), sometimes a noun with a qualifier ('The Wide Skirt', 'Herbert Truczinski's Back' or 'Bebra's Theatre at the Front'). Phrases that are more elaborate, narrative or interrogative are the exceptions, such as 'Tapered at the Foot End', referring to the design of Oskar's mother's coffin, 'He Lies in Saspe', which reveals the whereabouts of Jan Bronski's unmarked grave, or 'Should I or Should I Not?', in which Oskar debates whether or not to recommence his interrupted growth.

Grass once said in an interview that what he found so fascinating about *Moby Dick* was Melville's 'addiction to the object', and he similarly produces poetic meaning from words designating things.[5] The 'wide skirt' of his first chapter heading belongs to Oskar's grandmother Anna Bronski, a peasant who keeps warm by wearing four skirts at once, each week casting the one that she has worn closest to her skin into the wash and putting on a clean one to show to the world. This memorable sartorial fact somehow sums up both her life and character. Her skirt is also a synecdoche for her own sexuality and for motherhood in general. When Oskar's future grandfather, the Polish nationalist Joseph Koljaiczek who is being pursued by the Prussian police for arson (we would nowadays have to call him a terrorist), hides under her skirts, which is the novel's first fantastic conceit, he finds more than safety, according to the grandson who spends his life searching for similar womb-like spaces to shelter from a threatening world. It is an elemental meeting of earth and fire, the twin principles of movement and immobility.

The Tin Drum is also an artist's novel or *künstlerroman*, another distinctive German genre, which recounts how a practitioner of a particular art form was shaped by his background. It is exemplified by Gottfried Keller's *Green Heinrich*, which Grass read in childhood and reread while writing his first novel. Given Oskar's background at a nexus of persecution and violence, it may seem strange that Grass should devote time and energy to matters pertaining to art. Yet Grass almost always writes about art or literature, artists or writers, or he deploys fictional writers as narrators. In fact literature about literature would become something of a stock in trade, as he reflects on the status of his own reflection of the world. It can also be a sign of the characters' selfishness, as is certainly the case with Oskar, or wish to escape to a world in which only his or her self-fulfilment is what counts. In *Peeling the Onion* Grass recounts how he dedicated his own life after the end of the war to sating his three hungers: for food, for sex and for art. A more immediate model than Keller, however, is Mann's *Doctor Faustus* (1947), which is a novel about the German nation and its fatal pact with the devil told through the biography of an avant-garde composer.

The Tin Drum is also about mourning the dead. Oskar attends a number of funerals and he loses family members, first his mother, then both his 'putative fathers', the Polish Bronski at the beginning of the war and the German Matzerath at the end, as well as Markus, who is sometimes counted as a third Jewish father.[6] Oskar recounts the deaths of the love of his life, the Liliputian Roswitha Raguna, who gets blown up by a shell in France, and the greengrocer Herr Greff, who hangs himself when he hears the news that his favourite pathfinder Horst Donath has been killed on the Eastern Front and he receives a letter from the police on the subject of his interest in adolescent boys. Reports from the front that one after another of Oskar's contemporaries have 'copped it' pepper the second book. There is a carefully calibrated economy of death and suffering in *The Tin Drum*. Grass gives each individual and each grouping their due and builds up to a double crescendo in 1945: Oskar's nightmare of the merry-go-round which is powered by the Apollonian Goethe

Oskar (David Bennent), his stepmother and former girlfriend Maria (Katharina Thalbach) and Treblinka survivor Mariusz Fajngold (Wojciech Pszoniak) at the burial of Oskar's presumed father Alfred, in Schlöndorff's *The Tin Drum* (1979).

and the Dionysian Rasputin in memory of the children who were killed in the evacuation; and finally Fajngold's vision of the Jewish victims of Treblinka. The Jews thus have pride of place but the German civilians already receive their due.

The Tin Drum is the most famous German novel to be written after 1945. Success was repeated twenty years later when Volker Schlöndorff, a leading director in the New German Cinema Movement, took first the Palme d'Or at Cannes, then the Oscar for best foreign film at the Academy Awards. *The Tin Drum* was the first German film to win either coveted prize. Grass assisted in the adaptation, which is carried by the performance of twelve-year-old David Bennent as Oskar. Sadly, the film only covers the first two-thirds of the novel and plans to make a sequel once Bennent was old enough to play a larger Oskar came to nothing. The film's prominence came to mean that there have since been two versions of *The Tin Drum* in international circulation. Maria Sommer reports that at the dinner for former Nobel Laureates in 1999 in Stockholm, none had read the masterpiece by that year's winner but all ten had seen the film.[7]

Cat and Mouse

The nearest Pilenz comes to the haven of a psychiatric hospital is lodging in a *Kolpinghaus*, a hostel for working-class Catholic men, similar to the *caritasheim* where Grass himself lodged. Pilenz cannot settle down in a job or a relationship; he wants to believe in something, as he did in his youth, but he remains dissatisfied by what Cold War politics and religion have to offer. Grass invests Pilenz with rather more of his own biographical markers than Oskar. As well as the same year of birth and identical progress through the Nazi years in Danzig-Langfuhr, they also share literary ambitions, though Pilenz remains at 33 where Grass stopped being ten years his junior. Aged seventeen, Pilenz went a step further than Grass when he actively failed to help his friend Joachim Mahlke when he was on the run from the military, lying to him that he intended to return to check on his welfare if he hid out on the minesweeper where they had played three summers ago. He then wrongly convinced himself that his behaviour was somehow all right because Mahlke would come back to the water's surface after diving, just as he used to when they were children. Pilenz's guilt is more tangible than either Oskar's or Grass's own.

The object of Pilenz's fascination and wary friendship is Mahlke, who also shares some of Grass's background: a German-Polish Catholic family, expulsion from the Conradinum, war service as a tank-gunner and dedication to a cause. Like the Grass family after 1939, the Mahlkes suppress their Polish affiliation, but unlike Grass, Mahlke was expelled for a prank which was politically subversive – 'borrowing' the Knight's Cross belonging to a Conradinum alumnus who came back to his old school to give an inspiring talk about his bravery as a submariner. Mahlke discovered that the coveted medal was the perfect counterbalance to his troublesome Adam's apple, which causes him so much embarrassment, as he marched up and down with it dangling around his neck in front of his younger friends. In a gesture which shocked Nazi veterans, as it was supposed to do, Grass also describes him tying the medal to his half-excited penis. Yet in *Peeling the Onion*, Grass revealed that some of the spirit of the nameless young Jehovah's Witness who kept repeating 'we-don't-do-things-like-that' when presented with a gun during his labour service also fed into his depiction of Mahlke. The admission appears counter-intuitive because Mahlke very certainly did take up arms and developed a conscience only once he had destroyed the forty Soviet tanks he needed to win his medal.

Cat and Mouse has a message, which is another contrast with *The Tin Drum*. If Oskar was an artist first and a moralist second, for Pilenz the roles are reversed. His fable is dialectical rather than Aesopian (as the title may lead a reader to assume) because the roles are anything but clear-cut. In the Aesopian fable the clever mice get the better of the cat, which only has superior strength on his side. In the Grimms' fairy tale 'The Cat and Mouse in Partnership', however, the mouse ends up in the cat's belly. Grass was a lifelong reader of the brothers Grimm.

Mahlke plays both roles; he is both aggressor, who wins the highest military medal his country can give him, and a victim, always being toyed with by his contemporaries and higher social and cultural forces which get him in the end. He wants both to conform and to gain recognition in order to distract attention from his uncontrollable, outsized Adam's apple. On the first page a passing cat is said by Pilenz to become fascinated by the movements made by the sleeping Mahlke's throat and pounces on it, waking him up with a jolt and leaving him with a scratch. Or did Pilenz or one of the other boys draw the cat's attention to Mahlke's mouse? Pilenz only half answers his own question, knowing merely that one of them was involved and that this is the reason he has to write. In *Dog Years*, the psychology underpinning a similar relationship produces Matern and Amsel (Aryan and Jew) and Tulla and Jenny (Aryan and Gypsy). Each time the perpetrator is vindictive and brutal, the victim is sensitive, innocent and artistically inclined. While the role played by Pilenz is more ambiguous than that of Matern or Tulla, Malhke is emphatically no Amsel or Jenny. He places his talents at the service of the Nazis and returns aged eighteen as a decorated war hero. Yet he is ultimately a victim of the same Nazi war machine when he takes his own life rather than be executed for deserting from the army. Mahlke deserts, so we must assume, because he has realized the truth about wartime heroism and come to understand that he was sold a lie at school. Excelling as a young Nazi soldier was a compensatory gesture. When his former headmaster refuses to allow him to address the school on the grounds that he was once expelled, Mahlke lies in wait for him on his way home and beats him up. With Pilenz's assistance he then repairs to the minesweeper, in the knowledge that he now counts as a deserter for overrunning his leave and would be executed if caught.

By designating *Cat and Mouse* 'a novella', Grass is applying the formal definition of another classical genre, which he also read as a child. As always in Grass's fiction, and as was typical in novellas, there is a narrative frame, making the teller and the telling of the tale as central as the tale itself. The reader needs to wonder who Pilenz is and why he is relating this recollected story of his wartime love–hate friendship with a more remarkable and slightly older boy. Pilenz is making an honest enough attempt to dredge up an account of this haunting encounter from his adolescence, just as Mahlke retrieves trophies from the half-submerged Polish minesweeper. He is not exactly unreliable, although he lies to Mahlke in their final crucial scene, but he is not completely straight either. Sometimes he is no longer sure what happened or what his role in the events was. When he reports the arrest of Herr Brunies, who we will learn in *Dog Years* died in Stutthof, Pilenz can only comment that he hopes 'not to have given evidence against him' (IV:41).

In a meta-fictional feint which has always delighted literary critics, Pilenz admits at the outset to his own fictionality: both he and his story are themselves embedded in a further invisible frame by the author 'who invented me because that is his job' (IV:6). There are further well-advertised allusions to the conventions of the novella. The succession of strange objects which Mahlke wears around his neck are leitmotifs associated with nineteenth-century German versions of the genre by Storm, Keller and Droste-Hülshoff. Grass also incorporates a possible 'turning point' (Mahlke's temporary theft of a Ritterkreuz, which announces his decision to win one of his own) and an 'extraordinary event' (his desertion), which according to Goethe defined the novella. Yet for all its classical characteristics, *Cat and Mouse* is a fragment, consisting of thirteen sections and beginning *in medias res* with three dots and lacking a conclusive ending. Grass shows once again that literature cannot offer closure and literary perfection can no longer console readers for their dissatisfactions in the material world because, like religion, literary culture was implicated in the Holocaust.

Pilenz lets slip a handful of details about his own situation as a teenage boy. He is estranged from his parents and his family relations are mildly dysfunctional: while his father is absent at the front, his mother has taken up with another man. Meanwhile his elder brother has been killed in action and their mother appears to spend more time grieving for him than caring for her surviving younger son. Perhaps this is the reason why Pilenz has a diminished sense of himself. He is still constricted by adolescent modes of address learnt from his all-boys' school and does not even think to tell us his first name – we learn in *Dog Years* that it is Heini. Like his father, Pilenz feels that he has been pushed out and turns his anger on to 'the great Mahlke', as he and the other boys nickname him, by chiselling out his name from the work-service latrines, for example. Like a more successful older brother, Mahlke has been everywhere and done everything first. Pilenz is right to think that he has done it better.

Grass admits to borrowing the epithet 'great Mahlke' from Alain Fournier's *Le Grand Meaulnes*, in which a less successful surviving character reports on the life of an enigmatic contemporary he admires.[8] As the name Mahlke derives from the Polish for small (*mały*) the description is a contradiction in terms. Mahlke is highly devout, which inspires Pilenz to work as a server in church so that he can observe him; he is highly attractive to the opposite sex, as we find out when two girls from Berlin volunteer to urinate on the ice to help him break a hole through it in the middle of winter and later when we learn that he has had an affair with a sergeant's wife during his labour service. It is because of his superiority that he is isolated from his classmates, never really becoming one of the gang;

as one of them says to Pilenz, you would not be pleased if your sister showed an interest in him. Mahlke is different.

Cat and Mouse is Grass's most visual book and its most arresting image is that of tank-gunner Mahlke aiming his fire at a mental representation of the Black Madonna of Częstochowa, who in turn is holding a photograph of his father over her lap. The Black Madonna became Poland's patron saint after she rescued Polish forces by appearing above the besieged town of Częstochowa in a vision. Mahlke grew up with her image as well as a photograph of his father in work uniform after he and a colleague saved human lives in a rail crash. A portrait of Marshal Piłsudski is also on display at the family home, underlining their Polish affiliations. In order to destroy each tank, Mahlke must fire at an image of everything which he and his family cherish most: his father, his religion, his Polish heritage and a substitute object of sexual desire. This is, so the reader must assume, the essence of the speech he wanted to give to the boys at the Conradinum, which would have contrasted with the homilies delivered by the two winners he listened to as a boy.

Cat and Mouse was usually admitted by Grass's fiercest critics to be a worthy successor to *The Tin Drum* and was well received on publication in 1961. But it is more combative than his first novel and in some ways angrier. Grass knew that he was taking on the veterans' associations and deliberately provoked them by associating military heroism with adolescent phallic display. He was pursued by Kurt Ziesel, an old Nazi activist, who eventually won the right to call him 'a pornographer' because of passages in the novella. *Cat and Mouse* was the first of Grass's works to be made into a film, by the new-wave director Hansjürgen Pohland, one of the signatories of the 1962 Oberhausen Manifesto, which called for an end to the consensual 'Papa's Kino' of the post-war years. Pohland cast cabaret author and performer Wolfgang Neuss as the adult Pilenz returning to Gdańsk, where he recreates the formative episodes of his youth, interacting with the adolescent friends of his

memory. It is a highly intelligent literary adaptation which deserves
to be better known but on account of difficulties in its production,
Grass himself never championed it.[9]

Dog Years

Dog Years occupies a strange position in Grass's oeuvre. He insisted
right to the end of his life that his second novel was more important
to him than the public's favourite, *The Tin Drum*,[10] sometimes
expressing frustration that it stood in his first novel's shadow.[11]
There are a number of outward similarities. Both novels have three
books, corresponding roughly to the pre-war, war and post-war
periods, each time the first two are set in Danzig and the third
in the Rhineland area of West Germany. But *Dog Years* does not
provide aesthetic pleasure in the same way as *The Tin Drum*. It is a
more abstract novel, more allegorical, and more fragmentary. The
narrator Liebenau calls it 'rhyme-less' because it offers no aesthetic
closure and cannot wrap up the past neatly, any more than Pilenz
was able to provide an ending to his tale. For Michael Minden
it is a philosophical novel, invoking Adorno and Horkheimer,
Schopenhauer and Thomas Mann, which Grass wrote 'in order
to resist the canonization of *Die Blechtrommel* as the culminating
novel of Vergangenheitsbewältigung'[12] and to draw attention to the
inadequacy of literature or art to address Nazism. Grass imagines
that the mountain of bones in Stutthof was visible to the naked eye.
Stutthof was integrated into the network of local roads and railways,
but while Tulla confirms that the bones are those of human beings,
Störtebeker can only imitate the modish pseudo-Heideggerian
jargon in response to them.

It is unusual for a novelist to go over the same material in the
same chronological sequence for a second time. Rushdie wrote
that *Dog Years* taught him: 'When you've done it once, start all over

again and do it better.' For Rushdie this meant that he had to return to the subject-matter of *Midnight's Children* (1981) in *Shame* (1983), but *Shame* is about the history of post-Independence Pakistan while *Midnight's Children* was about India.[13] Grass returned to his Danzig material for aesthetic, moral and philosophical reasons. His second novel is not a sequel to his first but a rewriting of it. When he mentions Oskar Matzerath repeatedly in his subsequent fiction, he does so essentially for reasons of self-reference. *Dog Years*, in contrast, was never quite finished in his mind. Rats take on the role of dogs as the false other of human beings in the novel of the apocalypse entitled *The Rat*, for example.[14] In *Too Far Afield*, he once again employs a team of narrators.

Two years before his death, Grass prepared extensive artwork for a fiftieth-anniversary edition which was published in three handsomely produced hardbacks in 2013. The 120 engravings, transferred to paper by his long-time collaborator G. Fritz Margull, took almost as long to complete as the original novel. They are visual illustrations of textual motifs which remained as fresh in Grass's mind as they were in the early 1960s.[15] The equivalent commemoration of *The Tin Drum* in 2009 came from outside, in the form of a book of essays published by the Lübeck Grass Haus, which also mounted an exhibition.[16] The main concern in the run-up to the anniversary was to commission new translations, which resulted in a special translators' conference in Gdańsk.[17]

Dog Years' narrators, particularly Amsel and Matern, eschew the first person, which signals both a distance from their emotions and a disconnect with their readers. They reveal their characters through their deeds and their encounters with others or interactions with external objects. In a way it is misleading to call them 'narrators'. The author of the first brief monograph on Grass suggests 'ghost writers' because they each take on a task which ultimately is assigned to them by Grass, the author, who once again discreetly indicates their fictionality.[18] *Dog Years* is led by rhythm as much as story, by the sounds of the words and their morphological textures, as well as the smells and tastes of the objects, animals and activities which are depicted. Grass starts with the concrete or the visual and either explores how they acquire meaning through association with context or lets them stand by themselves and invites the reader to wonder what to do with them. There are fewer anecdotes, asides and explanations than in *The Tin Drum* and more extended sequences and fantastic setpieces which rely on the accumulation of unusual vocabulary for their effect. The humorous tone is more measured, though the irony sometimes all the sharper, while the metaphors can be as obscure as they are in Grass's early poetry and drama. In the first sequence, for example, the key object is a penknife which the young Matern throws into the mighty Vistula, near to the point where it flows into the sea – also the place where he lives. At first the object looked like a stone and Grass follows Matern by using the dialect term *zellack*, but Matern gradually comes round to owning up that it was a penknife. The significance of Matern's gesture of violently ridding himself of the knife is that he and Amsel had used it to swear 'blood brotherhood', which Matern now regrets. He is not an articulate character, always expressing himself in deeds rather than words; by casting the penknife into the water he is reneging on his oath of friendship with the small, fat, probably half-Jewish boy with artistic inclinations who hitherto had enjoyed his protection.

There are passages of poetic prose which challenge readers' sensibilities, such as the pointless killing of crows, rats or frogs; Amsel's ingestion of body parts of various amphibian creatures (which he is able to regurgitate after holding them in his stomach, thus distracting attention from his inability to do sport); or the seven-year-old Tulla mourning her drowned brother by assuming the life of a dog. The reader is spared no detail in her later inducing of a miscarriage. Other narrative sequences extend over many pages, such as the ritual beatings-up of Amsel and Jenny by Matern and

Tulla's thugs, the escape of the dog Prince from the Führer's bunker or the final sequence down Amsel's underground scarecrow factory.

Dog Years is about reacting to horror, suffering or witnessing persecution, and participating in it just because it is going on and you can. The title metaphor concerns both time and definitions of 'doggish' behaviour. A year in the life of a dog is seven in the life of a human being, which is one reason in 1963 that the recent Nazi past is not likely to be over any time soon. The dogs in question – Harras and Prince – are German Shepherds and are bred by Matern's family, who live downstream from Danzig at the delta of the Vistula. Liebenau's family, who own a timber business in Langfuhr, like Grass's paternal grandparents, acquire Harras from the Materns in 1927. On the eve of the war, the dog is poisoned by Matern. It is human beings rather than dogs who behave 'like animals'. Harras sired Prince, who is presented to the Führer on his birthday in 1934 – then ten years later to the day, in frustration at the way that the war and his business is going, Liebenau's father destroys Harras's old kennel with an axe. Prince was brought back to Danzig on a visit with his new owner in September 1939 as the city got swallowed up into the Reich. The Liebenaus, along with the owners of Prince's mother, Thekla, are invited to meet Hitler in the Grand Hotel at Zopot. As the Führer turns out to be too busy to see them, their request to be presented to Prince instead is granted; as they respectfully gaze at him through a window, they remark how his features resemble those of his parents. Grass is interested to show, through this obviously untypical connection, that the two families – and by extension their friends and neighbours, Tulla and the trio of victims, Amsel, and Jenny and Papa Brunies – are linked not so much with high politics but with the ideology of the regime. According to the most famous sentence in the novel, everything which happened under the Nazis also happened or could have happened in the suburb of Langfuhr. This is why 'The dog is central.'

Matern is usually designated the 'perpetrator' in the novel, with Amsel as the 'victim' and Liebenau the bystander or *mitläufer*. The distinctions only work up to a point. As an artist, Amsel acquires a new identity after his near fatal beating-up and prospers as an impresario in Berlin for the rest of the Nazi period, becoming a leading exponent of post-war success in the Federal Republic. Liebenau, who probably has more in common with Grass than any other character in his fiction, is too young to be tested. After the war, he does take a job in broadcasting, which Grass once said that he could easily have done himself, to the certain detriment of his ambitions to become a writer.

For all its emphasis on aesthetics and literary self-reflection, *Dog Years* marks a shift towards ideas and historical cause and effect. The third book includes an extended allegory of the Economic Miracle, for which Grass consulted the SPD's future finance minister Karl Schiller. His only comment was that Grass had underestimated the role of the banks, which after the financial crisis of 2008 Grass would quote with some glee. *Dog Years* addresses Nazi crimes more directly and wants to force a response from its readers. In episodes such as the intercalated dialogue about the miracle spectacles, which enable their wearers to see into the past of whomsoever they are looking at and to compare what they did during the recent doggish period with what they said they did, Grass is striking a more overtly didactic pose. He also presented the episode as a one-act play, *Thirty-two Teeth*. In other ways, too, his literary work was becoming more social democratic, which was a trend that was set to continue.

Dog Years gave some readers the impression that only method now really counted. After hearing Grass read from his manuscript at the Gruppe 47 in 1962, Johannes Bobrowksi wrote that, 'the conceit, the motif, or the theme become ends in themselves, their success as art, as literary experiments, is all that counts and all that you are left with is an artistic product.'[19] The last line, 'Every man bathes by himself' ('*Jeder badet für sich*'), may be more portentous

Grass with Johannes Bobrowski, 1963.

than meaningful. The novel has never been made into a film or adapted for the stage (apart from by Grass himself) and unlike *The Tin Drum* and *Cat and Mouse* was also not associated with controversy or scandal. When Grass was elected to the Berlin Academy of Arts the year it was published, Martin Heidegger quietly resigned, but it was only after Heidegger's death that it emerged he had taken offence at the parodies of his philosophical language, which some of the characters use as an excuse for Nazi atrocities. There are at least two German novels which react to *Dog Years*, however. Bobrowksi distances *Levin's Mill* from its epic pretentions, insisting that his smaller novel deals to greater effect with a more localized incident.[20] In 1971 the émigré Edgar Hilsenrath's *The Nazi and the Hairdresser* takes the binary between 'German' (Matern) and 'Jew' (Amsel), which Grass adapted from nineteenth-century anti-Semitic literature, a stage further, showing how the anti-Semite needs 'the Jew' as an inversion of his own ideal identity.[21] Furthermore Hilsenrath gives the Jew Itzig Finkelstein blond hair and blue eyes and the Aryan ss-man Max Schulz a hooked nose, but Finkelstein and his family are all murdered in the Holocaust and the novel is narrated by the surviving mass murderer Schulz, who assumes his old school-friend's identity and emigrates to Israel under his name. This afterlife makes *Dog Years* arguably a more German novel than *The Tin Drum*, whose literary legacy through novelists such as Rushdie, Irving and Gabriel Garcia Marquez was international.

Local Anaesthetic

Prior to publication in August 1969, Grass recognized that *Local Anaesthetic* was a transitional work and that Eberhard Starusch, his forty-year-old bachelor narrator who has recently retrained to become a teacher of 'German and thus also history', was no Oskar or Amsel, although Grass as author would be judged with reference to the two bigger earlier novels. He called *Local Anaesthetic* the sort of novel which authors sometimes write more for themselves, comparing it with Mann's follow-up to *Buddenbrooks*, *Royal Highness*, which is not ranked among his masterpieces, and *Lotte in Weimar*, which is – even if it lacks the epic breadth of *The Magic Mountain* and *Doctor Faustus* and for that reason stands in their shadow.[22] If Mann was in his thoughts once more, then he must have remembered the middle-aged Thomas Buddenbrook, who dies 'of a tooth' after a visit to the dentist which coincides with an encounter with Schopenhauer's *The World as Will and Idea*. After atypically immersing himself in this dark work, Mann's respectable merchant no longer recognizes that life has any meaning and suddenly collapses. *Local Anaesthetic* is also about toothache as a metaphor for existential pain, but Starusch is a fighter who discusses the Stoicism of Seneca with his dentist rather than letting himself be overcome by the pessimism of thinkers such as Schopenhauer.

The cover image depicts a finger hovering too close over the naked flame of a candle. *Local Anaesthetic* is about controlling feelings and repressing hatred, which is transformed in Starusch's mouth into plaque, one of the causes of his dental problems. Struggling to manage his anger, he fantasizes about murdering a former fiancée and their child because she has been unfaithful. He also mulls over his role as seventeen-year-old gang leader Störtebeker in late 1944. This past life enables him to understand the seventeen-year-olds in his class who protest against intolerable injustice, in particular the war in Vietnam. Scherbaum has a plan to shake the smug West Berliners out of their indifference to the suffering in Vietnam by dousing his pet dachshund Max in petrol and setting him on fire on the city's main thoroughfare, the Kurfürstendamm, right in front of Café Kranzler, where fur-coated ladies of a certain age gather to eat cream cake. His teacher's mission in the second of the novel's three sections is to persuade Scherbaum of the virtues and efficaciousness of peaceful protest and democratic engagement. As Grass's most direct treatment of the West German student movement, this central part of *Local Anaesthetic*, which was also performed on the Berlin stage as *Before* in advance of the novel's publication, has received the most critical attention.

As a novel about the student movement, *Local Anaesthetic* was highly topical. Grass was not far from the centre of the action: the anarchist Kommune 1 was founded in February 1967 next door to his family house in Niedstraße, in a flat sublet by Uwe Johnson, who was away in New York. After their plan to shower the visiting American vice-president, Hubert Humphrey, in cake mixture, which went down in history as the 'pudding attack' when the police made arrests following a tip-off, Johnson asked Grass to oversee their evacuation on 8 April. In June that year the communards went on trial for incitement to arson following the publication of a satirical leaflet. Grass was now witness for the defence, explaining that their statements, which he clearly had little time for, were in the tradition of the Futurists and the Dadaists and could not be taken as serious calls to set buildings on fire.[23] Time would prove him wrong on that point. Grass had also worked with Gudrun Ensslin in the 1965 election campaign when the young scholarship student of German literature, who became a founder of the Red Army Faction, or Baader-Meinhof Group, five years later, joined the Election Workshop of German Writers to help the SPD with slogans and soundbites. Shortly before Easter 1968 she and Andreas Baader planted two home-made explosive devices in two Frankfurt department stores. The bombs exploded in the middle of the night, injuring nobody but causing serious damage. As Grass was finishing *Local Anaesthetic*, his one-time acolyte was thus serving a prison sentence for arson, which she had committed for the same reason that Scherbaum wanted to burn his dog – the idea in both cases being that the public would get a sense of what it was like when a creature or a building was set on fire and thus empathize with the Vietnamese.

The other strand of *Local Anaesthetic*, about Starusch's failed engagement in the mid-1950s, takes up an equal amount of space in the novel and is narrated in a more challenging way. Starusch is in the dentist's chair throughout (the treatment on his lower jaw extends over several days in February) and is either speaking to his dentist or telling stories to himself in the form of invented film scenarios, which enables him to alternate between first- and third-person narration. There is a television on in the background of the dentist's surgery which is supposed to distract the patients and encourages Starusch to see past versions of himself on the screen. One can also read these passages as notes for a novel which is first mentioned in the last paragraph as 'The Gesture of Pulling Through – or the Case of Schörner', after the Wehrmacht general who mercilessly enforced Hitler's order to fight to the last man.[24]

Whether planned autobiographical novel or imaginary film of his past, the veracity of everything that Starusch narrates here is questioned in the novel's third section when he returns to the dentist for a new round of treatment. The dentist now claims that he has ascertained that it was not Starusch's fiancée Linde who was unfaithful with Schlottau, an employee in the family firm who served with her father in the war, but Starusch who was caught in bed with Schlottau's wife, which resulted in his getting fired after Schlottau got his revenge by tipping a lorry load of concrete over his soft-top Mercedes. Starusch, moreover, was a serial philanderer and had earlier lied about his status in the cement business which belonged to Linde's family. In Starusch's version there are three men: Starusch himself, the electrician Schlottau and Ferdinand Krings, Linde's father, who exist in relation to each other through their relationships with Linde. Krings is based on Schörner and returns home after ten years in a Soviet POW camp to a mixed reception from family and fellow countrymen. Grass's original title for *Local Anaesthetic* was *Lost Battles* because Krings/Schörner refights the defeat on the Eastern Front in his mind, according to the novel, a common reaction among the German military. Schlottau is obsessed, in Starusch's version, with avenging himself on Krings because as his former commanding officer Krings demoted him to private. Somehow in Starusch's mind this motivates Linde and Schlottau to start an affair, which justifies Starusch's murderous fantasies.

There are all sorts of gaps in Starusch's biography, which is almost as contradictory as Matern's. He recounts at length his time as Störtebeker but does not say how he ended up in 1945 in a POW camp in Bad Aibling, the same camp as Grass himself. Was he in the Wehrmacht, like Schlottau and Krings, or a different wing of the German military, like Grass? Why is Starusch not angry with Krings as the worst kind of unrepentant military leader and post-war *mittelstand* industrialist?

Local Anaesthetic depends on the technique of doubling to make sense: Schlottau not Starusch wants revenge on Krings and Starusch's colleague Irmgard Seifert has a wartime secret that could match Starusch's, not to mention Grass's own. In her mother's attic, Seifert discovers letters which she wrote as a troop leader of the *Bund Deutscher Mädel* (the version of the Hitlerjugend for girls) extolling the virtues of the regime. She also reported a farmer for refusing to co-operate in the digging out of anti-tank defences on his land. Nothing happened to the farmer but that does not diminish the import of Seifert's denunciation.

Seifert and Starusch, both still single at forty, have an on-off engagement and are both obsessed with the past and the activities of the younger generation, on whom they project their fears, failures and fantasies of compensation. Scherbaum and his classmate Vero Lewand, meanwhile, seem content by the end to settle for conventionality. She drops out of school to marry a Canadian linguist, while he works out for himself that his dramatic plan was not the right way forward after finding the example of a seventeen-year-old anti-Nazi resistor executed in 1942. His middle-aged teacher's advice was at best a prompt. The novel was wrong about the younger generation, many of whom took up to a decade before they were ready to embrace the values of the republic, but right to demonstrate hopefulness. The month after publication saw Willy Brandt scrape home in national elections to form a governing coalition with the Free Democrat Party (FDP) and become the first SPD chancellor since Hermann Müller in 1930.

3

Public Uses of Fame:
Willy Brandt and the SPD

German biographers of Günter Grass gasp at how famous their subject became after the publication of *The Tin Drum*, which passed half a million sales after a mere five years and was but the first in a string of best-sellers which has extended beyond his death.[1] Heinrich Vormweg, who worked closely with Grass between 1976 and 1980 as editor of the quarterly *L76*, recalls how Grass claimed to have affected the consumption of eels, the popularity of moustaches and the perception of pornography.[2] Volker Neuhaus in 1997 entitles a chapter of his biography 'World Fame', quoting sales figures from the USA which show that by the 1980s more copies of *The Tin Drum* had been sold than of the original, *Die Blechtrommel*.[3] Neuhaus goes further in 2010, contending that Grass is one of only three German writers who achieved such international renown with their first novels, the other two being Mann with *Buddenbrooks* and Goethe with *The Sufferings of Young Werther*.[4] Meanwhile, in 2002 Michael Jürgs noted that Grass was the first German from the sphere of culture to appear on the cover of *Time* magazine (which he did in April 1970); when *Local Anaesthetic* came out later that year it made a greater impact than the original *örtlich betäubt*.[5] In 2006 Harro Zimmermann reports a finding of the Allensbach Institute that more than 80 per cent of West Germans in 1979 knew the names of Günter Grass and Heinrich Böll. Two years later *The Tin Drum* and *The Flounder* were found to be the two best-known German novels among American college and university students.[6] Grass's

Helen Wolff (1906–1994), in 1979.

fiction was celebrated across the Western world and won him major prizes in France, Italy and Spain, while the Eastern bloc paid him the negative compliment of banning his books: though a samizdat translation circulated from the early 1970s, *The Tin Drum* was not published in Polish until 1984, the same year that the first of his books (*The Meeting in Telgte*) was made available to readers in the GDR.

A key element in Grass's domestic standing was clearly his renown in the United States. Grass conquered America in the same way as the Beatles and Dylan Thomas. In Ralph Manheim's translations, he read like an American novelist who could write from first-hand experience about that most fascinating and enduring of contemporary topics: Nazi Germany. He first visited America in 1964 at the invitation of his publishers, sailing on the SS *Bremen* with Anna, and stayed for three weeks. He would return on many occasions over the next 43 years, reading frequently at the New York Goethe House or Goethe-Institut, on university campuses, in 1966 at Princeton where the Gruppe 47 held its penultimate meeting, and finally presenting *Peeling the Onion* with Norman Mailer at New York Public Library in 2007. Grass was helped, until her death in 1994, by the shrewd advice of his New York-based publisher Helen Wolff, whose husband Kurt Wolff had offered him a contract for a translation of his first novel before it was published in German. After Kurt's death in 1963, Helen organized translations – Manheim for prose and drama, Michael Hamburger for poetry, sometimes stand-ins for essays which she often recommended shortening or annotating and placed by choice in outlets such as *The Nation*, the *New York Times* and the *New York Review of Books*. It is no accident that Grass's correspondence with Wolff, which they sustained over three decades, is his richest exchange. She also introduced him to academics, including Hannah Arendt, as well as scholars of German literature, critics and American writers. While her praise of each new manuscript was calculated and they clashed over Ronald

Reagan in the early 1980s, there is every sign that her admiration for his accomplishments as man and writer was genuine.

By the end of the 1960s Grass was also being deployed as a much-needed asset of soft power. He visited Israel in March 1967, reporting back at length to Willy Brandt, now foreign minister and deputy chancellor in a grand coalition between the CDU and the SPD. He accompanied Brandt as chancellor on his historically most symbolic mission to Warsaw in December 1970, to sign a treaty recognizing the Oder-Neisse Line (on behalf of the Federal Republic) as the German-Polish border and the concomitant loss of the eastern provinces. In June 1973 they travelled together to Israel on the first state visit. Grass reported back on other trips, such as that to Prague with Anna in March 1968. Brandt believed that Grass achieved more for German-Yugoslav relations in a visit to Belgrade in May the following year than he could imagine anyone else doing.[7] After Brandt stepped down as chancellor in May 1974, the two men attended the first post-Franco conference of the Spanish socialist party together in December 1976.[8] Grass continued in this role as semi-official cultural ambassador up to the last decade of his life.

Grass cultivated his fame as assiduously as he had sought it in the first place. He enjoyed prestige among the public because he had faced up unflinchingly to the recent past in his novels and was prepared to speak truth to power. Grass wanted to admit guilt, express regret and face up to Nazi criminality and the majority's complicity in it. He was also good on television, loved performing his own words and nearly always relished attention. As the Federal Republic began to conduct the kind of serious conversation with itself about the nature of the new democracy and the meaning of the Nazi legacy, Grass was determined to lead debates. Through the 1960s, he wanted the FRG to recognize its post-war borders, to take responsibility for the inhabitants of the GDR as fellow Germans, to make it unacceptable for prominent ex-Nazis to occupy high office, and to legalize women's control over their reproductive functions.

Willy Brandt in Warsaw in December 1970, kneeling at the memorial to the victims of the Ghetto Uprising.

As well as picking his causes, Grass expressed himself eloquently and demonstrated an innate sense of timing and theatre. He also surfed a political wave between the federal elections of 1961 and 1969, representing the 'better Germany' which was respected abroad, elements of which first congregated in the Gruppe 47. It was a generational battle in which Grass (still only 42 in 1969 when Brandt became chancellor) learnt to project the passion of youth.

There is a myth in Grass biography, however, that it came as a surprise in 1961 that he should volunteer to help Brandt and the SPD by improving speeches, working on slogans, supplying ideas and, once it came to the next elections in 1965, mounting a one-man parallel campaign in support of Brandt. The originator of this myth was Grass's mentor, the host of the Gruppe 47, Hans Werner Richter, who wrote in his memoirs that he would not have thought to take Grass along to the meeting with Brandt on 5 September 1961, had Brandt not requested his presence.[9] The myth proved powerful because of the apparent mismatch between *The Tin Drum*, an anarchic, obscene, blasphemous and even nihilist novel, and conventional understanding of social democracy. Grass's loyalty seemed to be to his art and Oskar's choice of a musical instrument over a practical vocation emblematic of his author's own priorities. Yet Grass's first novel and the decision to campaign for Brandt were both born of a dissatisfaction with the state that the world was in. He entitled his last volume of political essays *Rolling Rocks*, connecting his endeavours as a citizen in the public realm with the metaphysics of Sisyphean existentialism, which had fascinated him as a young man.[10] Trying to make the world a better place was as hopeless a task as forever pushing a boulder to the summit of a mountain only to see it tumble back down again. A number of his early poems and dramas are moreover already overtly political (*The Wicked Cooks* is a straightforward allegory). The metaphysics in such pieces as *Ten More Minutes to Buffalo* can be contextualized historically, just as Beckett's absurdist masterpieces were always taken as profoundly realist in totalitarian societies and, like Grass's writings, banned as a result.

It was anyway wrong to call Grass an apolitical writer, as Richter himself must have known. Before the historic first meeting with Brandt, Grass contributed an article to Martin Walser's paperback entitled *The Alternative, or Do We Need a New Government*?[11] Grass apostrophizes 'the lukewarm, well-behaved, angry SPD, auntie SPD, my bad conscience, source of my irritation, my weakly founded hope for the future' (XI:36) and ends by asserting that Goethe would be voting for Carlo Schmid, one of the authors of both the FRG's Basic Law or Grundgesetz in 1949 and the SPD's Bad Godesberg programme in 1959, when the party distanced itself for good from Marxism. As ever in his thinking, writers already represented the 'better Germany'.

Grass's stated reason for returning to West Berlin in January 1960 was to experience at first hand the geopolitical reality of division at the height of the Cold War.[12] 'I greet Berlin' is the first line of the opening poem in *Gleisdreieck*, which is called

Konrad Adenauer, Federal Chancellor, 1949–63.

after a station on the under- and overground rail network. Berlin was where history was being made, in deed and word. Günter and Anna were there on 17 June 1953 when the Soviet high command ordered in the tanks to crush a protest over pay by construction workers. In the West, Konrad Adenauer made out that it was a popular uprising against communism; in the East, Walter Ulbricht

Grass with Ingeborg Bachmann (centre) at the Filmtreffen (Conference on Film), 1962.

insisted it was a counter-revolution. In *The Rat*, Grass called them both 'counterfeiters' and the 1950s a 'false decade'. He wrote his most successful play, *The Plebeians Rehearse the Uprising*, to demonstrate his thesis about the events of that memorable and tragic day.

Grass liked mixing with like-minded artists, intellectuals and politicians. The truncated former capital may have lost its historic centre in the East, not to mention its entire hinterland, which was now part of the GDR, along with its status as the seat of power, but it proved attractive to the new creative classes, who were encouraged to settle and work there. In the second half of the 1960s, it became the centre of the student movement and anti-Vietnam War campaigns. Grass moved in the key literary circles, supported Höllerer at the newly founded Literarisches Colloquium Berlin on the banks of the Wannsee and, at various times, lived near to fellow novelists Johnson, Bachmann and Frisch, enjoying close friendships with the poet Peter Rühmkorf, radical publisher Klaus Wagenbach and left-wing journalist Ulrike Meinhof. Grass organized tirelessly, was angry when fellow writers showed less enthusiasm for the SPD (the subject of his Büchner Prize acceptance speech in 1965) and continued to write prolifically, not just prose fiction, but poetry (*Gleisdreieck* in 1960; *Questioned Out* in 1967) and plays.

Brandt was a kindred spirit and natural ally. He sought out the company of artists and intellectuals, wrote books himself and recommended that Grass complete his political education by reading the works of the SPD's first leader, another politician-cum-writer, August Bebel. Bebel's *Woman and Socialism* would become a source for *The Flounder* and his autobiography one of several models for *Peeling the Onion*. Grass would come to see one of his roles in the SPD as being to encourage party activists and elected representatives to know their SPD history and see their own endeavours in an historical context. Bebel never held office but Brandt inherited both his pocketwatch, as Grass notes in *From the Diary of a Snail*, and his reformist agenda. *The Flounder* includes a treatment of the so-called 'revisionism debate' in the 1890s as German social democrats drew up battle lines between revolutionaries and reformers. A key episode takes place at Bebel's funeral in 1913, coincidentally the year of Brandt's birth, which double centenary in 2013 Grass marked with a handsome publication containing accounts by contemporary SPD politicians of what Bebel's legacy meant to them.[13] Four chapters of *My Century* are devoted to party history. *From the Diary of a Snail* and *Grimms' Words* also record Grass's experiences on the campaign trail.

There was lots to be angry about in the Federal Republic. In politics, the media, business and the judiciary, old Nazis were back. They voted for Adenauer, like the ex-soldiers in *The Tin Drum* who are still pursuing an escapee from Danzig's Polish Post Office. Because economic reconstruction and the battle against communism – one of the arguments for supporting Hitler in the first place – now took pride of place, there was no general reckoning with Nazism. If Grass was impressed by Brandt, he was incensed when, just days after the building of the Berlin Wall, Adenauer attacked Brandt for leaving Nazi Germany in his 'Brandt alias Frahm' speech. 'Willy Brandt' was a code name adopted in the anti-Nazi resistance in Norway, which, so Adenauer hoped his voters would conclude, showed Brandt to have been a traitor to the fatherland. Adenauer also kept Hans Globke, the author of the Nuremberg Race Laws, in a leading civil service post. The majority of the population was in denial about the

Willy Brandt, *c.* 1969.

deportations of Jews from their midst and the atrocities committed in the name of Germany in the hundreds of concentration camps built in the countries occupied by Hitler's forces. Social attitudes and the language used to express them had barely evolved. On top of all this, there was a fiction which was repeated by all major political parties that the pre-war territories which Germany lost in 1945, mainly to Poland (Pomerania, Silesia, West and East Prussia) but also to the Soviet Union itself (Königsberg), would somehow be reclaimed and the expellees, such as Grass's own family, permitted to return. Electing Brandt, the anti-Nazi resistor, at the head of an SPD-led government would at a stroke offer a corrective to all this, or so Grass argued through two gruelling election campaigns.

By working for Brandt and persuading others to support his policy of dialogue with the Soviet Bloc or *Ostpolitik*, Grass was compensating for the past in general as well as his own. Brandt, fourteen years his senior, boasted the perfect anti-Nazi back story, which Grass summarized in a key speech from 1965 which he entitled simply 'In Praise of Willy'. Even as an adolescent in the dying days of Weimar, and in contrast to the teenaged Grass, Brandt took the right decisions. Aged nineteen in 1933, he fled Nazi Germany to Scandinavia to carry on the fight; he participated in the Spanish Civil War and returned to Germany after the Second World War in a Norwegian uniform which subsequently in the eyes of his critics indicated less his support of democracy than his allegiance to a foreign power. Brandt was one of a series of professional friends who became substitute parent figures for the young Grass as he was making his mark on the new republic: Hans Werner Richter (1908–1993) was undoubtedly the first, Helen Wolff (1906–1994) the most attentive (and she shared a first name with his mother as Brandt did with his father), his publisher at Luchterhand, Eduard Reifferscheid (1899–1992) another.

Grass's first cause was not the SPD, however, but the lack of freedom of expression in the GDR, his first public statement uttered not on the election stump but at the University of Leipzig on 21 March 1961 when he passed on the best wishes of the former Leipzig student, and his friend, the young writer Uwe Johnson. He then read 'The Stockturm. Long-distance Song Effects' from *The Tin Drum*, in which Oskar shrieks his disgust at the state of moral corruption in Danzig and breaks the windows of the municipal theatre. The chapter was not chosen at random. Johnson had been obliged to move to the West in 1959 to publish *Suppositions about Jacob*, which after *The Tin Drum* was the second literary sensation of the year. Johnson's best wishes were rejected by a party official who spoke directly to the audience, which included the academics Ernst Bloch and Hans Mayer, who would both soon follow Johnson to the West (Bloch in 1961, Mayer in 1963), and the future playwright Volker Braun.[14]

Two months later, in May 1961, Grass accepted an invitation to the fifth Writers' Congress in East Berlin. In his intervention he punctured the self-satisfaction of the culture minister, who had declared the GDR superior to the West in the literary field, by once again drawing attention to Johnson's novel and praising a number of contemporary Western authors whose works were also not available in the GDR.[15] It was this intervention which resulted in Brandt's request to Richter that Grass attend a meeting between Brandt and sympathetic writers on 5 September 1961. Brandt recalls that he and Grass had already been introduced in Berlin in the late 1950s at the house of some Swedish friends.[16]

It was thus the absence of freedom of expression in the GDR in particular and the German question more generally which brought Grass into politics. In his tour of the country in 1965 one of the main reasons he gives for voting out the Christian-Democrat-led coalition, now under Ludwig Erhard after Adenauer's retirement in 1963, was its failure to stand by the population of the GDR, choosing the Western alliance over unification. In 1965 he gave five speeches at 52 meetings in more than thirty towns and cities, choosing areas in which the party was traditionally weak. In *My Century* he imagines

Grass with Uwe Johnson at Tempelhof Airport, Berlin, 1963.

reporting on his journey to Richter: 'I'm learning so much, Hans, uncovering mould which has been collecting for so long, in communities where they are still fighting the Thirty Years' War' (IX:209). In 1969, when Brandt was finally successful, Grass spoke at even more election rallies and found that the reception was often more welcoming.

Grass's speeches were designed to be experienced live, but he also published them as illustrated pamphlets with the look and feel of literary manifestos, which he sold at his election rallies. The speeches take different forms, containing a mixture of policy ideas, anecdotes, personal reflections, *ad hominem* polemics and history lessons. They can be entirely whimsical, such as his suggestion that new cities called New-Danzig, New-Breslau and New-Königsberg be built for the expellees so that their dialects can be passed on to future generations. There are common threads, such as appeals to the Enlightenment and a wish that German voters would learn to participate in democracy by expressing views, voicing protest and working out the truth for themselves rather than taking statements on trust from figures in authority. The history lessons are about the Weimar Republic, which failed politically, so Grass believed, because it had too few supporters and because the extremes, either left wing or right wing, with their all-encompassing explanations, appeared superficially more attractive.

After ditching their commitment to Marxism, the Social Democrats were very much a reformist rather than a revolutionary party. According to Grass, they were never satisfied with the status quo but prepared only to edge their way forward, expecting to be knocked back and to encounter moments of 'stasis in progress'. According to a theory he articulated in *From the Diary of a Snail*, social democracy had two enemies, one of which he called 'melancholy', a tendency to slump into resignation because of the apparent absence of change, the other 'utopia', an expectation that a perfect society can be created. If this is a political philosophy, then it is slightly quirky and could be embodied by just about any democratic party. Its purpose was to rationalize and justify his grass-roots campaigning; praxis, for Grass, thus came before theory.

From the beginning Grass was also concerned to define his role as a poet and novelist who intervened in politics against the background of writers' entangled allegiances to ideologies and regimes in the modern epoch. This subject preoccupied him throughout his career and is a major theme in his principal works from *The Flounder* to *Grimms' Words*. He studied the history of writers and politics (Brecht and Benn, Sartre and Camus), determined to avoid pitfalls which had ensnared Weimar leftists. In 1969 he worked alongside the academic Kurt Sontheimer, author of two classic studies, one on Thomas Mann and national politics and the other on the failure of the Weimar democracy.[17] Weimar was a lesson in how not to do it, but if Grass had a role model, it was

Thomas Mann, who was all the more powerful a presence for being unacknowledged.

Grass insisted that he neither placed his art in the service of a cause, as his colleagues in the GDR were obliged to do, nor did he impart wisdom by dint of his vocation as a writer, as Romantics from Shelley to Stefan George claimed they could do. Instead, when he spoke at an election meeting or published an article in a newspaper, he did so as a citizen; similarly, when he published a volume of poems or wrote a novel, he left his politics behind. At the end of *From the Diary of a Snail*, he explained the distinction with reference to two beer mats, one representing writing and the other politics. While he can move the beer mats about independently, they can also be placed one on top of the other. The analogy is banal and the distinction between writer and citizen can easily be unpicked: it was only because he was the author of internationally acclaimed fiction that the public gave him a hearing and they were bound to bear in mind his pronouncements of policy when they read his poetry.

At the outset, Grass was moreover something of a *bürgerschreck*, or terror of the bourgeoisie, a time-honoured role in European letters since Baudelaire in 1840s Paris or even the *Sturm und Drang* in 1770s Germany. In a notorious case, the parliament of the city of Bremen overturned a decision in January 1960 to award Grass the prestigious Bremen Literature Prize for *The Tin Drum* on the grounds that 'some chapters of the work should be put on the index of writings likely to corrupt youth.'[18] The first scandal of his literary career boosted his growing reputation: Kurt Wolff predicted it was worth the 8,000 DM in lost prize money.[19] Throughout the 1960s he was pursued through the courts on charges of obscenity and blasphemy, but Grass revelled in the public vilification, which sometimes led to disturbances at his meetings during his 1965 election tour. He was less pleased in September that year when his front door was set on fire by Sudetenland activists angered that he was advocating that Germany give up its claim to their homeland. Then came the gift of condemnation from the federal chancellor himself. In an 'Open Letter to Ludwig Erhard' in May 1965 Grass criticized government policy towards Israel, which the republic did not recognize diplomatically for fear of alienating the Arab states. Grass claimed that the dead of Auschwitz and Treblinka were thereby insulted and in response Erhard made some highly derogatory remarks about Grass which included a reference to 'degeneracy in modern art'.[20]

Brandt tested Grass's loyalty in December 1966 when Erhard stepped down and the SPD was offered the role of junior partner in a grand coalition of the two major parties. Grass pleaded with him in a public exchange of letters not to accept the position of deputy to the CDU's Kurt Georg Kiesinger, an NSDAP member from 1933 to 1945 and Foreign Ministry official during the war, responsible for monitoring foreign broadcasters and liaison with Goebbels's

Grass after the arson attack on his house, 13 Niedstrasse, Berlin, 1965.

13 Niedstrasse, Friedenau, Berlin. Anna and Günter acquired the house for their growing family in 1963.

Ministry of Propaganda. Such a move also gave the opposition no voice in the Bundestag and risked alienating the growing number of younger generation radicals from parliamentary politics. Grass was right on the second point. His own energies were increasingly taken up with countering the appeal of radicals enthused by student leader Rudi Dutschke, some of whom by the late 1960s were openly calling for the violent overthrow of the state. The frontier city of West Berlin became increasingly polarized over the rest of the decade, but between the generations rather than between ethnic groups as in Danzig before the war. The young protested against the Vietnam War because they thought that the Americans were behaving like the Germans in the Second World War, while the bulk of West Berliners were grateful to the same American military for guaranteeing their freedom. Grass even addressed Dutschke's Vietnam Congress in February 1968. He followed the dictates of his head rather than his heart.

In May 1968, when French students brought Paris to a standstill and briefly looked poised to take the reins of power, Golo Mann suggested that Grass become mayor of West Berlin. Heinrich Albertz had resigned in the wake of the police shooting of a student during the demonstration against the shah of Iran on 2 June 1967. Only Grass, according to Golo Mann, could relate to disaffected German youth. Anna, who yearned to return to the bohemian anonymity of the early years of their marriage, called the idea 'repellent' (*abscheulich*) in a letter to Uwe Johnson,but her husband was disappointed that the SPD did not take it up.[21] He expressed his frustration to party manager Egon Bahr, who had evidently let him know Brandt did not want him to be a candidate for the Bundestag either. Grass expressed the wish to take charge of international development in an SPD-led government, but Grass knew this was unlikely to happen: 'I can see it coming . . . I will carry on writing one book after the other and, even though I am heartily sick of the topic, producing thoughts about intellectuals [*geist*] and power [*macht*].'[22] After Brandt became chancellor, Grass indicated once more that he wanted a different sort of political role, exploiting his international reputation, perhaps working with countries in the developing world through the newly created ministry for economic co-operation.[23] Brandt eventually replied with a number of lower-key suggestions, including opening a new Goethe-Institut in Australia, visiting the newly founded Nehru University in Delhi and taking responsibility for the surviving German-speaking communities in South America.[24] Grass was obliged to take the hint and never raised the matter again. Brandt treated writers and intellectuals seriously, seeking their advice (without Grass's interest in the developing world he may never have written the *North–South Report*) and working to keep them onside, but he did not want novelists as ministers or even members of the Bundestag. He was equally unimpressed, now no longer chancellor but still chairman of the SPD, by Grass's suggestion that his novelist colleague Siegfried Lenz stand for the presidency in 1980.[25]

Up to 1969, Grass was on the side of history, cajoling the voters to move in directions which a majority eventually showed they were ready to adopt. He continued to offer advice to the SPD, whether it was solicited or not, hitting the campaign trail again in 1972 when Brandt was re-elected with a thumping majority, but he was not always certain how he should negotiate the switch from opposition to government. One thing was for sure: he wanted to carry on making a difference and did not consider that his work was done.

Whether Grass would have made a decent minister or mayor of West Berlin is moot but his speeches and correspondence with leading SPD politicians show that he had an appetite for the minutiae of policy. He was interested in the 'travails of the plains', as Brecht termed the challenges of everyday politics which came after the excitement of revolutionary struggle. But Grass's flair was for publicity. He could grab a headline, force an issue into the public eye, or, in an election campaign, take the fight to the opposition and argue with wavering voters in beer halls or market squares. His friend and Berlin neighbour, the Swiss author Max Frisch, who portrayed 'Germany's Günter Grass' as an ever-present media phenomenon in a section of his *Diaries*, privately expressed his misgivings in a journal entry dated 14 February 1974.[26] By this time Grass had criticized Brandt's political leadership on national television. According to Frisch, barely a week would go by without

Participants at the 1961 meeting of the Gruppe 47. Looking back at the camera: Wolfgang Hildesheimer (left) and Siegfried Lenz (right).

an 'encyclical' on one subject or another, as Grass is always ready to give an interview or an off-the-cuff quote when a journalist calls, seemingly needing to see his name on the front page, preferably at the expense of the likes of Henry Kissinger.[27]

Grass soon found more time for his writing, of course, which he had never given up, but there was a temptation to trade in past glories. *The Meeting in Telgte*, published in 1979, is a lyrical exercise in controlled nostalgia; in *Grimms' Words* from 2010 he celebrates his lifetime's campaigning achievements by selecting encounters exclusively from the decade between 1965 and 1975. *From the Diary of a Snail* was the first such memoir, recording the historic 'change in power' in 1969, which began in March when Gustav Heinemann became federal president on the third round of voting and by the narrowest of margins. The choice the following autumn between Brandt and Kiesinger for chancellor could not have been more symbolic and the combined forces of SPD and FDP only narrowly outnumbered the CDU. Grass had good reason to believe that without his interventions the outcome would have been different; certainly no one campaigned harder than he did. His tours

Grass with Max Frisch, 1975.

eventually became the stuff of political folklore. In 1997 his driver Friedhelm Drautzburg opened a chain of politically themed bistros on the back of his association with the tour called the *Ständige Vertretung* (the 'permanent representation', the name given to the embassy which was not an embassy run by the Federal Republic in East Berlin). In 2011 Grass's 1969 campaign became the subject of a celebratory book of reminiscences and photographs.[28]

4

Back to the Future, Forward
to the Past

With Brandt re-elected in 1972, and this time with an overwhelming majority, Grass needed new themes and new professional challenges. He also wanted to reaffirm his literary reputation. Not all critics shared his view that *Dog Years* was a better novel than *The Tin Drum*. His two plays written in the 1960s were not well received and he may have quietly acknowledged that critics who claimed *The Plebeians Rehearse the Uprising* was a brilliant idea inadequately realized had a point. After the stage version of the middle section of *Local Anaesthetic*, he never wrote for the theatre again. His third volume of poems, *Questioned Out*, published in 1967, mixes political verse with his trademark allegories, rich in visual and plastic imagery and often expressed through what Dieter Stolz has termed 'a private complex of motifs'.[1] While it is now fashionable to praise Grass's poetry as his enduring literary achievement, Grass was always judged on his prose fiction. *From the Diary of a Snail* is an insightful multi-stranded narrative essay, full of reflections on the SPD and the 1969 victory in the context of twentieth-century German history, especially the persecution of the Jews in the Third Reich, but it has little of the wit or invention which drew the world's attention to its author a little over a decade earlier.

Grass's private life was also becoming ever more complicated and he needed a new big novel for financial reasons. His marriage with Anna was suffering from the distractions afforded him by his fame, his prolonged absences and, reading between the lines, his serial infidelity. His first poem on marital discord, included in *Questioned Out*, dates from 1965. In *From the Diary of a Snail* he hints that Anna was in love with the Czech translator of *The Tin Drum*, Vladimir Kafka, whom he and Anna visited together in June 1969. Kafka's unexpected death from a brain tumour on 19 October 1970 overwhelmed both of them. In letters to Eva Figes, with whom he became closer at this time, he mentions that Anna's new boyfriend, who was only 26, behaved like one of the children and did not like having the paterfamilias around the house in Friedenau. At one point around 1975 husband and wife decided to divide 13 Niedstrasse – a rambling detached property built of distinctive red brick which they acquired for a song in late 1963 as house prices in West Berlin tumbled after the building of the Wall – with an inside wall down the middle. In 1973 Grass had set up house in Wewelsfleth with Veronika Schröter, an SPD party organizer who managed the Voters' Initiative for the 1972 elections, but he returned to Niedstrasse regularly, to see his four children and to attend to business. Schröter gave birth to a daughter in June 1974 whom they christened Helene after her paternal grandmother, but their attempt at living together was fraught from the start. The central exchanges in *The Flounder* between the nameless male narrator and his wife Ilsebill, whose pregnancy provides the novel with its nine-month narrative frame, are drawn from this ultimately unhappy liaison.

Read for encoded information on the state of the Grass marriage, *Local Anaesthetic* is more disturbing than *The Flounder*. If Anna read her husband's books, what was she to make of Starusch fantasizing about killing his fiancée and her child (not to mention the fate of the ballerina Jenny in *Dog Years*)? Grass lends a number of their biographical markers to Eberhard Starusch and Sieglinde Krings. Starusch is born the same year as Grass and Sieglinde is the same age as Anna. They get engaged (though never marry) in 1954, the year in which Grass and Anna married. Sieglinde's family are

Veronika Schröter in Wewelsfleth, *c.* 1973.

wealthy and the marriage would represent a great advance in
socio-economic terms for the young would-be son-in-law. In
Starusch's version, Sieglinde is unfaithful to him, but according
to the dentist it is Starusch who has a string of girlfriends. He is of
Cassubian stock (on both sides of the family) and when he returns
for the first time to Danzig (in 1955, rather than Grass's own date of
1958) he is greeted by an elderly female relative with the same words
that Grass's great aunt uttered to greet him. Starusch lost his mother
when her evacuating ship hit a mine in January 1945, but he talks to
her in his mind still – like most male characters in Grass's fiction,
Starusch does not have a significant relationship with his father
(the disreputable Walter Matern is the partial exception here).

Ute Grunert in Wewelsfleth, 1985.

The Flounder is indirectly inspired by lots of romantic friendships and one-night stands. The narrator knows all the main women in every historical epoch intimately and has slept with each member of the 'Feminal', the feminist tribunal which puts the fairy-tale fish on trial for propagating the male order down the ages. It is a novel about multiple mirroring and doubling: each female figure from the past, from the three-breasted Stone-Age Aua to the twentieth-century Polish Maria, is matched by a woman in the present. The auto-fictional narrator, meanwhile, sees himself reflected in all the men, playing multiple roles in each epoch, just as he recognizes Ilsebill pre-incarnated in each of the historical women. The novel ends at a point of uncertainty with the ejection of the controlling narrator from his position of epistemological authority.

The unsuccessful relationship with Schröter, following on so closely from a failed marriage and the resultant itinerant existence, taught Grass to value domestic stability, not least because it facilitated creative work. He did not enjoy settled circumstances again until May 1979 when he married Ute Grunert, who would play the role of steadfast partner for the following 36 years. Ute brought two young sons to the marriage and Grass's own younger son opted to live with his father once he was re-established in the half-timbered, seventeenth-century house in Wewelsfleth, which Susanne Schadlich, the daughter of the writer Hans-Joachim Schadlich, who took his family to stay with Grass on fleeing the GDR in 1977, recalls was ideal for children to play in: there was 'a lobby which used to be a pharmacy, lots of rooms like a doll's house with alcoves where we could hide'.[2] Grass's domestic situation was not completely settled, however. He had recently become a father for the sixth time, from a brief relationship with an editor at Luchterhand called Ingrid Krüger. It took a few years before he introduced this daughter to her half-siblings, the oldest of whom, twins, were by now 22. Just as his ideal of marriage excluded monogamy, he was not the most devoted fan of the nuclear family. On becoming a grandfather in 1984 he dreamt that he was an oriental patriarch surrounded by his progeny; more disturbingly, in his dream he was responsible for impregnating his eldest daughter, Laura.[3] He liked to be photographed with his ever growing brood, publishing the photographs in his *Studio Reports*. He invited them all to Stockholm in 1999 to witness his award of the Nobel Prize.

There were other reasons for valuing a settled life. Grass witnessed a number of his writer friends self-destruct. The theatre and film director Walter Henn, to whom he posthumously dedicated *Dog Years*, fell victim to pneumonia while serving a prison sentence for drunk driving in 1963. Henn was to direct the film adaptation of *Cat and Mouse* and he and Grass also discussed a film together about 'Father's Day', an exclusively male occasion which takes place each year on Ascension Day and which became the subject of the notorious eighth chapter of *The Flounder*. Paul Celan, the difficult friend who helped him with *The Tin Drum*, killed himself in 1970. Three years later Ingeborg Bachmann died in a house fire while living alone in Rome. Uwe Johnson would drink himself to death in Kent in 1984. None was capable of sustaining a relationship and each died before their life's work was complete. Like Johannes Bobrowski, they all failed to reach fifty, Grass's age two months after he published *The Flounder*.

The Flounder was written also against the background of second-wave feminism in West Germany and includes a number of caricatures of feminists and lesbians which continue to cause offence.[4] Grass was voted *pascha des monats* or 'male chauvinist of the month' by the new magazine *Emma* shortly after publication. His argument with feminism is a continuation of that with the student radicals, and more philosophically minded critics see the male–female binary in the new novel to be essentially metaphorical.[5] That may be so, but Grass's sexual imagination stands in the twentieth-century tradition which earlier produced D. H. Lawrence and Henry Miller, whose novels were still subject to censorship when Grass wrote *The Tin Drum* but were under assault for their sexist assumptions by the 1970s. *The Flounder* pushes at boundaries in slightly different ways. It is first and foremost an epic treatment of Danzig and thus also national history, through cooking and eating and also through the lens of what Grass understands to be sexual politics. His take is traditional to the extent that the battle between the sexes has been a staple literary topic since antiquity. Grass cites Boccaccio, but his main point of literary reference is the Grimms' fairy tale 'Of the Fisherman and His Wife', which he uses as a kind of narrative archetype showing how women's desires are responsible for the imperfect state of the world and the unhappiness of mankind. Grass at once inverts it by presenting women as the injured party throughout history and then attempts to collapse the sex binary altogether.

Grass spent some five years researching and writing *The Flounder*, which is longer than he ever spent on any other single project (*The Tin Drum*, *Dog Years* and *Too Far Afield* all took around three years each). When he had finished, he was confident that it was good and that it contained everything 'which is in me and which makes me who I am'.[6] It was a book about all things born of a wish 'to stick the world between two book-covers'.[7] As he was correcting the proofs he was still sure that 'the book is good' but after publication in August 1977, when it quickly exhausted its initial print run of 150,000, he expressed the fear that he would have difficulty producing something as many-layered as this fairy tale in future.[8]

Some of the novel's motifs had a long pedigree in his oeuvre. Eating and drinking, including the enumeration of ingredients of half-forgotten peasant dishes and the pre-modern culinary habits of the Danzigers he knew as a child, were prominent features in his early poetry. Grass took particular delight in using up those parts of pigs and cows (heads, innards, feet) which never found their way onto the tables of the wealthy and which nowadays tend to be discarded. Food was both an abiding passion and recuperative pastime since the days of hunger he experienced in the POW camp in Bad Aibling. It is a source of sensual pleasure, much like sex, which both reminds us of our animal nature and which, for the moment of our enjoyment, cancels out our mortality. In *The Tin Drum* you can tell what a character is like by what he or she eats. The malign force which governs that novel is embodied by the '*schwarze Köchin*', or 'dark cook' (or 'black witch' in Manheim's translation). Grass invests meaning in meals: Oskar is never so content as when he eats spaghetti with Klepp because, despite the unhygienic state of the utensils in the latter's Düsseldorf bedsit, the pair are friends.[9] Grass conjures a rather different atmosphere in *Dog Years* when just after the war Matern visits his former SA commander Jochen Sawatzki and new bride Inge and finds them boiling sugar beets to make syrup which they intend to sell. The nauseously sweet smell hangs heavily in the air inhaled by the trio of former Nazis.

Grass was by most accounts a generous host who believed in the power of conviviality to persuade guests to exchange experiences and interact with each other in ways which were inconceivable in other contexts. In his view, fellow writers practise solidarity by breaking bread together. Grass prepared lentil soups at some of the East Berlin writers meetings which took place in the 1970s. He took charge of the catering at Walter Höllerer's wedding in 1965. Only Reich-Ranicki went on record to say that he did not enjoy the fish soup which Grass cooked for him in lieu of a share of the royalties for *From the Diary of a Snail*. Reich-Ranicki's lack of culinary pleasure in the occasion was, as he well knew, a distinctly Grassian reaction to the difficult situation.[10]

Other components in the big new work can also be traced to Grass's beginnings as a writer and artist. His first representations of a flounder (in chalk and bronze) date to 1955, for instance.[11] In a note from 1961 he outlines an idea for an account of 'Father's Day'.[12] *The Flounder* is also the most Danzig-centred of all his books. In *Grimms' Words* he compares his continued fascination with his native city with James Joyce's concentration on Dublin and William Faulkner's on the fictional Yoknapatawpha County in America's Deep South. Since his first return in May 1958, he visited Gdańsk frequently, forming new friendships such as that with Bolesław Fac, a Cassubian shipyard worker turned writer whose account of industrial unrest in 1970 fed into the last chapter of *The Flounder*.[13] Grass was in Gdańsk in 1975 to make a documentary about the rebuilding of the historic old city, which he contrasted with the trend in West Germany to replace centuries-old bombed-out buildings with anonymous concrete.[14]

The Flounder retells the history of the Teutonic Knights' rule in Danzig, the alternating ascendancy of the Polish crown and the

Grass with Anna at the wedding of Walter Höllerer and Renate Margoldt, 1965. Grass took charge of the kitchen.

German-speaking Prussians, the French occupation at the time of Napoleon (who makes a brief appearance in the novel stopping over en route to Moscow, as does a weary Frederick the Great of Prussia) and the emergence of the nation state in the nineteenth century. Grass presents a new version of the life of the thirteenth-century Dorothea von Montau, the only one of the eleven female cooks who really existed, and makes novel characters out of an array of well-known male Danzigers or visitors to the city: Adalbert of Prague, Swantopolk, Jakob Hegge, Eberhard Ferber, Stefan Bathory, Martin Opitz, Governor Rapp and Pastor Blech are all figures from the city's history whom Grass grew up with. Most get a passing mention in *Dog Years*. Paul Simson's classic 1903 history of Danzig lay on Grass's desk as he was writing *The Tin Drum*: the ship's figurehead nicknamed Niobe was stolen by pirates along with the city's most famous painting, Hans Memling's triptych of the Last Judgement, which hangs to this day in Gdańsk's National Museum, the history of which is relayed by Simson.[15] The baroque painter Anton Möller, who now shares the attentions of Agnes Kurbiella with the poet

'Eva and the Flounder', etching of Eva Figes, London, 1976.

Opitz, and the revolutionary Friedrich Bartholdy are first discussed
in *Local Anaesthetic*. Möller gets into trouble for modelling an
allegory of sin on a local prostitute as his fiancée suspects correctly
that he has been unfaithful with her, while Bartholdy is already a
negative example of a seventeen-year-old revolutionary hot-head.
The Flounder at the same time challenges accounts of Danzig
and West Prussian history which championed the claims of one
group (usually 'the Germans' or 'the Poles') over another. Danzig's
origins are international. As its character was shaped by trade
and migration, its history has to be multi-voiced. *The Flounder*
is a novel about Germany and German history but presents the
uniform German nation state as the root of modern ills. It is the first
instalment of Grass's argument with nineteenth-century Prussia,
the second being *Too Far Afield*, his major literary response to
unification. Yet for Nicole Casanova, who accompanied Grass on
his reading tour in the autumn of 1977, he is showing more patience
with 'mother Germany' and readier to listen to her answers than he

was in the earlier fiction.[16] This dialogue will enter a third and final phase in *Too Far Afield*.

Other sources are more important for the novel's conceptual framework. Grass's idea of a harmonious prehistoric society where both goods and sexual partners were shared until men discovered their role in siring children is explored by August Bebel in *Woman and Socialism* (1879). Bebel builds on the work of Friedrich Engels but draws too on ancient Greek literature and the Old Testament to link the subjugation of the workers under capitalism to the subordination of women under patriarchy.[17] As a Marxist, he works with a triadic historical structure, positing that we are heading in the direction of a new society in which oppression will be lifted once again. Bebel's great work is cited in *The Flounder* in which the working-class cook Lena Stubbe is delegated to attend his funeral in Zurich in 1913 as representative of her local branch of the SPD.

Grass cannot quite connect all his characters with Danzig. Amanda Woyke, who encouraged the peasants to grow potatoes instead of millet, corresponds with the great Sir Benjamin Thompson in Bavaria. In a central and justly celebrated chapter the brothers Grimm discuss the fairy tale 'Of the Fisherman and His Wife' with the painter Philipp Otto Runge, who claims that he heard it in two versions from an old woman on the tiny island of Oehe near Rügen, and the writers Clemens and Bettina Brentano and Achim von Arnim. This fictional meeting takes place outside the city at the house of the cook Sophie Rotzoll. The chapter is called 'The Other Truth' for two reasons: it is a fictional addition to verifiable history and the brothers Grimm ultimately suppress the version of the fairy tale which casts the male sex in a poor light. Their falsification is emblematic of the skewed historiography which the novel exposes.

The only feminist writer to influence *The Flounder* was the Berlin-born British novelist and literary scholar Eva Figes. Her seminal *Patriarchal Attitudes* (1970) contains a number of insights which Grass includes: a female version of the Prometheus myth, for instance, in which woman first created the sun 'but kept back a little of the fire in order to cook, hiding the fire in her vagina when she was not using it';[18] and the idea that in prehistoric matrilineal society men did not understand their role in procreation until they were enlightened by a phallic-shaped serpent (a role played by the flounder in Grass's novel). Figes indicated that a dialogue took place between the two novelists by dedicating her novel *Seven Ages* to Grass in 1986. In *The Flounder* she is identified with the revolutionary Sophie Rotzoll, who tries to poison the French governor of Danzig with mushrooms (she narrowly misses but kills all six other dinner guests).

After first meeting on his 38th birthday in 1965 when Figes was sent to Berlin by *The Guardian* to interview him, Grass and Figes's friendship intensified at the beginning of the new decade, producing more than 100 letters over a thirty-year period.[19] Many of these coincided with the break-up of Grass's marriage to Anna and the ultimately unhappy association with Schröter, but the correspondence remained regular through the following decade. After his houses in both Berlin and Wewelsfleth became no-go areas, he fled to London in January 1976 to spend a fortnight with Figes and her two children while working on *The Flounder*. In *The Box*, he recalls that he was always packing up his typewriter and manuscript and that *The Flounder* was written pretty much on the hoof. He made an etching in London entitled 'Eva and the Flounder', drawn from a freshly bought fish which he then prepared for dinner.

When it came to domestic arrangements, Grass's own attitudes could also be distinctly patriarchal. Much as she esteemed his company, this seems to have been Figes's view, which she brought out in an interview on publication of the English version of *The Flounder*:

Figes: I think there is a problem posed by the new 'liberated' woman which neither of us has managed to resolve in our private lives. You once said to me 'What really matters is achievement'.

You have never lived with a woman who has put achievement first, and we both know that our sort of work involves a good deal of egotism. Do you think it is possible for a man and woman to live together as equals in that sense?

Grass: I think having children is in itself an important job.

...

Figes: The last time you were in England your life was in a mess, you felt misunderstood, and you said that you did not think bourgeois marriage was for people like us. When I said, 'suppose you were to live with a woman who wrote, and who had the same problems', you answered – to my surprise – 'No, too much competition'. Now surely, you of all people . . .[20]

The great writer needs a wife who will support him and put his work first. By October 1978 Grass had made up his mind that that wife could not be Eva Figes. In her *Seven Ages*, women control medicine (as witches) rather than cooking and take an ironic view of male achievements, most of which are fabricated in sagas to justify their absences from home and family.

The greatest contemporary political parallel is not explicitly mentioned in *The Flounder*. The trial of the Grimms' all-knowing talking fish parodies that of the leading members of the Red Army Faction (RAF) between May 1975 and April 1977 in a purpose-built wing of Stammheim prison in Stuttgart, thus coinciding with the latter phase of Grass's writing of the novel. The roles appear to be reversed, in that the patriarchal flounder is in the dock rather than the revolutionary terrorists, while his feminist accusers are the supposed radicals. Seeing as one of these feminists, Sieglinde Huntscha, took part in the atrocity of Father's Day, the women accusers in the Feminal are implicated in the historical catastrophe for which the flounder is arraigned. The terms of the trial are broadly speaking identical to that in Stammheim: on one side is a party supposedly guilty of crimes which include Nazism (the flounder in Grass's novel; the accusing West German state in the eyes of the RAF) and on the other side is a group of radicals turned extremists who in their efforts to oppose suffering appear to be aping their opponents' excesses (the lesbian perpetrators of Father's Day in *The Flounder*; the leading members of the RAF at Stammheim). As was noted in the last chapter, Grass worked with the young Gudrun Ensslin in the 1965 election campaign. In the late 1960s he was on friendlier terms with Ulrike Meinhof,[21] but he did not intervene in the often poisonous exchanges on the RAF leading up to the 1977 showdown between state and terrorists which became known as 'the German Autumn'. That autumn, in order to force the release of the RAF leadership, the industrial leader Hanns Martin Schleyer was kidnapped, his driver and bodyguards shot in cold blood. Instead of such intervention, Grass reflected the most dramatic subject of the decade in an epic work of fiction which appeared in the bookshops the month before the German Autumn reached its crescendo.

The Flounder now occupies an ambiguous place in his oeuvre. It was not often cited in the obituaries, but it inspired three British novels (Anthony Burgess's *Earthly Powers*, Lawrence Norfolk's *The Pope's Rhinoceros*, as well as Figes's *Seven Ages*), numerous PhDs and scholarly tomes, including three collections of essays in English within just over a decade of publication. It remained in Grass's mind, as poems in *Mayflies* and *Of All That Ends* both show. In 2007 a poll in Germany of 17,000 readers voted its first sentence 'Ilsebill salzte nach' the most beautiful opening sentence in German literature (the first sentence of Kafka's *Metamorphosis* got second place).[22] Needless to say, the beauty is rather lost in English translation, 'Ilsebill put on more salt', conveying only the physical action.

The Meeting in Telgte

The Meeting in Telgte only took nine months to write.[23] It grew out
of a section of the fourth chapter of *The Flounder* which imagines
a meeting between two poets in Danzig in 1636. One is Andreas
Gryphius, soon to become the most famous German sonneteer
of his age, whom Grass presents as a typically youthful firebrand,
and the other a world-weary Martin Opitz, the first theoretician of
German versification who has lately neglected poetry for his paid
employment as a diplomat (working possibly for two sides at once).
The pair discuss what poets should be doing to alleviate suffering in
the midst of a brutal war. According to Grass's poetics of alternative
history, which determine the narrative flows and counter-flows of
his novels, if such a meeting is not recorded in the history books, it
does not mean that it did not happen. It is up to novelists who 'fill
the gaps left in official history' (xii:180) to imagine what it could
have been like from a contemporary perspective. Grass asked the
leading scholar of the period, Albrecht Schöne, what the purpose
of an encounter between Gryphius and Opitz could have been:
'Did they argue? Did they get drunk? Did they have nothing to
say to each other beyond pleasantries?'[24] He is fascinated by what
Opitz, who as an Irenist was sworn to work for peace, was doing in
Danzig, seeing him as a prototype of the modern committed writer,
a representative of *geist* (spirit) who sought to exert an influence on
macht (power). Opitz reminded him of the twentieth-century pairing
of 'Brecht and Benn', which he develops in a chapter of *My Century*.[25]

The Meeting in Telgte depicts a similarly wholly fictional gathering
of writers, poets and publishers at the end of the Thirty Years' War.
It is a homage to the Gruppe 47 and dedicated to Hans Werner
Richter as a present for his seventieth birthday. It is the best example
of a favoured sub-theme in Grass's oeuvre, the role of the writer, both
vis-à-vis the reading public and in relation to power.[26] It is also his
most positive account of FRG history pre-1989. Gruppe 47 mythology

is woven into the history of the republic, the subject of both major books and attempts at revisionism (such as the false accusation that Richter and his associates were anti-Semitic, for instance, because they did not recognize the talent of Paul Celan in 1952).[27] Grass's early career and lifelong reputation were closely bound up with the group, and with *The Meeting in Telgte* he became one of its first and most influential chroniclers.[28] Through a work of fiction, he is once again writing history.

The Meeting in Telgte is thus an historical tale, set in 1647 (thus precisely 300 years before Richter sent out his first invitations) as peace negotiations between the exhausted great powers of continental Europe take place in the nearby cities of Münster and Osnabrück. Finally signed the following year, the Treaty of Westphalia saw France confirmed as the predominant force on the mainland in Europe. The German-speaking lands, on the other hand, loosely confederated in the Holy Roman Empire of the German Nation, lay in ruins and would take up to 200 years to recover their economic pre-eminence, the population reduced by half, those surviving traumatized, their cities sacked and countryside laid waste as foreign armies lived off the land for three decades. Grimmelshausen's *Simplician Writings* tell of every kind of cruelty inflicted on civilians and soldiers alike. The war remained in the popular memory until the time of Schiller, who wrote both a history of it and a trilogy of historical plays about one of its most famous commanders, Wallenstein, also the subject of an Expressionist epic written in the aftermath of the First World War by a novelist Grass claimed as his 'teacher' in 1967: Alfred Döblin. Like Grimmelshausen and Döblin, Grass prefers to present history as an 'absurd' sequence of events rather than to focus like Schiller on great men and destiny.

Scholars were impressed by Grass's knowledge in *The Flounder* of Grimmelshausen's sources for his famous description of the battle of Wittstock in chapter 27 of book 2 of *Simplicissimus*.[29]

He now emulates Grimmelshausen's rhetorical technique by artfully weaving quotations from Schöne's anthology of seventeenth-century German poetry into his account of the three days of readings.[30] Seventeenth-century literature had been a childhood interest. *Simplicissimus* leaves a mark on *The Tin Drum*, in which Herr Greff is a reader of the mystic poet Angelius Silesius, who takes part in the Telgte gathering. In a letter to his American translator, Grass elucidates a reference in *Dog Years* to Quirinius Kuhlmann, who was burned at the stake for heresy in Moscow in 1689.[31] Kuhlmann is too young to be invited to Telgte but in *The Flounder* Agnes Kurbiella follows him to Russia, where she meets a similar fate. Grass attests to Wolfgang Hildesheimer that he had been interested 'for years' in the composer Heinrich Schütz, who, after the Grimmelshausen-inspired figure of Gelnhausen, is the other great artist present at Telgte. Hildesheimer was finishing his novelistic biography of one the most written-about artist figures of all, Wolfgang Amadeus Mozart, and Grass points out that they face opposite challenges because there is so little material on Schütz, 'not even anecdotes'.[32]

The Meeting in Telgte is stylistically one of Grass's greatest achievements. The phrasing is elegant and sentences measured, the vocabulary drawn from the same lexical field, which contrasts somewhat with the preceding 'baggy monster' of a novel which is something of a textual patchwork. Now he maintains a consistent lightness of touch, striking a balance between high art and vulgarity, the comic and the serious, the real and the poetic. He deals most obviously with literary tradition and the history of the German language, but, bizarrely, while accepted as a supreme literary achievement, *The Meeting in Telgte* has not provoked much critical comment. After the sources were identified and readers accepted that the Telgte delegates did not have direct counterparts in the Gruppe 47 (with the exception of Dach as Richter and Gelnhausen/ Grimmelshausen as Grass himself), there remained only the question of the anonymous narrative voice.[33]

The Meeting in Telgte is designated an *erzählung,* or narrative, rather than a novella like *Cat and Mouse*, but it is a similar length and follows the classical criteria set down for a novella. Eduard Mörike's 1855 novella *Mozart on the Way to Prague* has a comparable theme and setting (in Mörike's case, the relationship between art and money and a country seat of the minor aristocracy). Grass has a clear and single focus (art and power) and recurrent motifs such as food and drink, the writers' thistle symbol and Dach's pumpkin gourd. He also has a turning point which follows on from the 'extraordinary event': when the writers are forced to realize that Gelnhausen has stolen their feast and probably killed its original owners. There is, moreover, a classical symmetry and simplicity to the structure. The action takes place over three days and two nights in an inn on a little island in the river Ems, similar to the often rural and out-of-the-way venues Richter chose (often because they were cheap) for the Gruppe 47 – Telgte itself being a site of pilgrimage lying roughly equidistant between the major cities of Osnabrück and Münster, where Europe's diplomats are engaging in a parallel set of talks. There are five phases in the collective mood which correspond to the dramatic arc of a classical play. In phase one the writers are pleased that they have arrived safely, that the meeting is happening and they have each been recognized through an invitation. Writers are vain individuals. In phase two, satisfaction gives way to disappointment when they dine badly that evening after fractious words have been exchanged in response to one or two disappointing readings. In phase three they are exulted when Gelnhausen leads them to believe that the feast has been donated in recognition of the significance of their endeavours (rather than stolen at musket point). In willed ignorance they gorge on:

> millet steamed in milk with raisins, bowls full of crystallized ginger, sweet pickles, plum butter, great jugs of red wine, dry goat cheese, and lastly the sheep's head . . . Into the mouth

Libuschka had wedged a large beet: she had encased the neck
in a gentlemanly white collar and transformed it with a crown
of marsh marigolds to preside o'er their feast. (VI:790)

Heinrich Schütz, an artist of genuine European rank, has by now
unexpectedly honoured them with his presence. Their hubris
precedes a fall in phase four when Schütz uncovers what really
happened and offers Gelnhausen advice about striking a balance
between fiction and truth, art and life. Schütz represents the views
of the Grass of the late 1970s just as Gelnhausen incarnates his
younger self. Grass depicts the collective mood once again through
attitudes to food: 'The festive board was a picture of desolation.
Piles of bones big and little. Puddles of wine. The formerly crowned,
now half-eaten sheep's head. The disgust. The burned-down candles.'
(VI:796) In the fifth and final phase, equipped with self-knowledge
after the departures of both Schütz and Gelnhausen, the survivors
agree on the words for a modest statement before the inn is burned
down and they are obliged to depart in disarray, their statement also
consumed in flames.

There are two immediate contexts for the tale in 1979. The more
obvious is indicated in the dedication to Richter: *The Meeting in
Telgte* is an appreciation of the achievements of the Gruppe 47,
which had met under Richter's aegis from 1947 to 1967. Richter
can reflect with Simon Dach that

Only words retained a sparkle where everything lay in ruins.
While the princes had debased themselves, poets enjoyed public
respect. They, in contrast to the powerful, could be certain of
immortality. (VII:713)

This confidence is dented somewhat by the events of the next
two days. Yet while, by the end, the writers can have no illusions
about their status in the world, there is no doubt that they represent

the 'better Germany' and that their works will be recognized by posterity even if they are ignored now. Their names do indeed live on through their words, while the wealthy ambassadors at the peace conference, along with most of their employers, have been forgotten. If the reader is to take away a thought from *The Meeting in Telgte* it is that writing rather than fighting is what counts in the longer term.

Grass was in a confident mood as 1978 drew to a close. In a letter to Brandt written just after he completed the manuscript, he proudly reports that 900 students turned out to hear him read the first two chapters of his latest book on a Saturday afternoon in Bonn and stayed on for an hour afterwards to discuss the contents with him. He then claims that next to the Latin Americans, German-language authors, from Austria and Switzerland and both German states, are currently producing the best literary writing in the world. German literature is the great success story of the post-war years, in Grass's opinion, outstripping achievements in other art forms or the arts and humanities in general. The years 1965 to 1973 marked a period of particularly fruitful dialogue and co-operation with politicians.[34]

Even making allowances for lobbying and his satisfaction at having written what critics will soon call a minor masterpiece, Grass is in danger of sounding smug. In *The Meeting in Telgte* he depicts himself, too, as Gelnhausen and Schütz, who have a better understanding of life than the others. Gelnhausen threatens to outshine his more experienced and better educated contemporaries schooled in rhetoric and composition when he combines his experience of the world with his literary learning in a linguistically rich account of the war which has just ended; Grimmelshausen did precisely this with his *Simplician* cycle of novels, just as Grass did with *The Tin Drum*. To underline his identification with Gelnhausen/Grimmelshausen, he lends Gelnhausen his own declaration of intent regarding his own first novel, which he published in 'Looking Back on *The Tin Drum*' in 1973.

There is, however, another, equally relevant context. Grass is also addressing the role of writers in a divided Germany and in Cold War Europe at the end of the first decade of *Ostpolitik* and more than thirty years after the end of the Second World War. In 1647, 1947 or 1979, the nation is politically sundered and occupied by foreign powers. Only their shared language binds Germans together. Grass was closely involved in cultural diplomacy with the GDR and other Soviet-bloc states through most of the 1970s, albeit in an independent capacity. He was an editor of the quarterly paperback *L76* which, according to its cover, published 'literary and political contributions' dedicated to 'democracy and socialism' and drew its authors from both sides of the iron curtain. As the FRG enacted anti-extremist legislation under the so-called Radicals Decree, requiring all state employees to swear an oath to the state, and sections of the media watched out for Baader-Meinhof sympathizers among the intelligentsia, there was a sense in the West that both German states were repressive in broadly comparable ways and consequently in need of similar reforms. Writers thus played similar roles, whether in the East or in the West.

In this spirit, Grass took part in a series of fifteen private meetings between East and West German writers which took place in East Berlin between May 1974 and November 1977. He gives a brief summary in *Headbirths* and makes the meetings the focus of a cluster of chapters in *My Century* ('1975', '1976' and '1977'). Hans Christoph Buch recalls that the question of a single German literature transcending the two German states always interested Grass, as he himself attests in *Headbirths*.[35] The rules were adapted from the Gruppe 47: the names of who should read from a work in progress were picked from a hat; there were fifteen minutes for the reading and fifteen for discussion; politics was off-limits. As they began in the afternoon and the West Berliners had to return across the border by midnight, not everyone could take a turn each time.[36] After the readings, there was food and drink and Grass in particular

Grass with Ute and Wolf Biermann, Niedstrasse, Berlin, 1976.

encouraged the host to cook a meal, recommending usually a
linsensuppe (lentil soup) – as his recipe for this dish included
generous portions of mutton, the choice was simple but not ascetic.

Grass attended each time and decided who to invite from the
West, preferring 'open minds', meaning neither dyed-in-the-wool
anti-communists nor apologists for the Soviet Union. Attendance
usually reached a dozen, with the East Berliners taking it in turns
to host, for both practical reasons and to keep the secret police
guessing. When the news got out that Max Frisch would be present
in November 1976, a month after the singer-songwriter Wolf

Biermann was stripped of his citizenship for comments made during a concert in Cologne, four of the most prominent GDR writers showed up at the house of the poet Günter Kunert: Stefan Heym, Heiner Müller, Christa Wolf and Jurek Becker.[37] The Biermann expulsion marks a turning point in GDR cultural politics. The meetings stopped a year later because the East Berliners had either left or were preparing to leave for the West. They thus ended in failure, like Simon Dach's fictional gathering; if there is a complacent undertone to *The Meeting in Telgte* in the West German context, in that of East Germany and Eastern Europe it represents a gesture of defiance.

The Meeting in Telgte, originally an occasional piece of writing in the baroque tradition, is the only prose work after *The Tin Drum* and *Cat and Mouse* which is critically accepted as an enduring work of German literature.[38] Grass continued to imagine how writers might reflect on their social role and what they could do to improve the state of the world. He also continued in his attempts to bring his colleagues together to discuss their writing in the spirit of the Gruppe 47. In 2005, after the renewed disappointment of electoral defeat when the seven-year Red–Green coalition was voted out, he initiated the Lübeck Writers' Meetings, which introduced millennials such as Eva Menasse and Benjamin Lebert both to the collegial practices of the Gruppe 47 and the contradictory personality of their greatest contemporary. It was his wish that the meetings continue after his death, which was granted for the first time in 2016.

5

Crying Wolf in 'Orwell's Decade'?

Grass predicted that the 1980s would be less productive than the decade just ended and this turned out to be true.[1] He realized that he needed a break from writing, having been busy on literary projects more or less non-stop for eight years. In this time he produced two minor works mixing essay and autobiography, *From the Diary of a Snail* and *Headbirths*, either side of two literary masterpieces, *The Flounder* and *The Meeting in Telgte*.[2] Settled once again in Wewelsfleth he returned to sculpture, which he called his 'first profession' and last practised all those years ago as an art student. From now on whenever he was between books, he would be working in clay and bronze, as well as drawing in charcoal, ink and pencil, and printing copper etchings and lithographs. His working partnership with the Berlin printer G. Fritz Margull dates from 1977. In 1995 Grass regained his mental equilibrium after the angry reception of *Too Far Afield* by rediscovering another old medium – watercolour – which he used to illustrate the mini-poems in *Lost and Found Items for Non-readers* and the 100 stories in *My Century*. Art served his writing in multiple ways.

In public life the 1980s would be anything but quiet. The catalyst was NATO's decision in December 1979 to negotiate for multilateral disarmament from 'a position of strength', by deploying new atomic missiles (Cruise and Pershing) at American bases in West Germany and the UK, in response to new Soviet ss-20 missiles stationed in the East. In the same month the USSR invaded Afghanistan. After

Ronald Reagan became president of the USA a year later, American politicians sometimes gave the impression of believing that a nuclear exchange in Europe was 'winnable'. Germans took to the streets to protest; opposition to nuclear rearmament was inscribed into the DNA of the new political party ostensibly dedicated to ecology, *die Grünen*, which was founded in 1980 and from then on competed with the SPD for left-of-centre voters.

'Orwell's Decade', as Grass pessimistically dubbed the 1980s (VII:70), began with the slim volume *Headbirths, or the Germans Are Dying Out*. It is a multi-stranded narrative essay which includes an imagined route through the Nazi years had he been born ten years earlier, a parallel life as the right-wing Christian Democrat Franz-Josef Strauss, and accounts of the East Berlin writers' meetings and a journey to the Far East with the film directors Volker Schlöndorff and Margarethe von Trotta. Grass explains his concept of the 'pastpresfuture', or *vergegenkunft*, a new temporal dimension which unites the present with both the past and the future. In *Headbirths* the real and imagined life stories are interspersed with essayistic fantasies. At one point the auto-fictional narrator wonders whether 'Germany' would cease to exist if the birth rate decreased further and Germans stopped having children altogether; at another he imagines that German authors from across the centuries pair up in a show of strength to the politicians (his partner would be the Romantic humourist Jean Paul). He also explains his plans were he to become dictator: he would replace compulsory schooling, which did him little good, with a system of travelling house tutors; oblige judges to serve 10 per cent of the custodial sentences they pass down; and train all citizens, including children, grandparents but also pets, to join a partisan army to defend the country against invaders. And the two German states would swap systems every ten years, allowing the GDR population to recover from socialist austerity and giving their FRG compatriots a chance to toughen up. A pan-German authority would meanwhile oversee the rolling return of private property and the expropriation of the sites of production.

This is the author as political fantasist rather than practical policy advisor. After at least a decade and a half dedicated to getting votes for the SPD, he is repositioning himself in the public imagination and satirizing his own posturing. The election speech and public lecture always offered him a chance to get a point across, to make a practical suggestion, to take a stand which can pull a debate in a particular direction or place an item on the news agenda, but he did not always do so with a completely straight face. In an address to the Club of Rome in 1989, for instance, he praised rickshaws, an Asian mode of transport which he witnessed in action on his travels, as a pollution-free solution to inner-city congestion, not to mention an answer to climate change. Three years later in *The Call of the Toad* the plan is put into effect by the British-Bengali businessman Mister Chatterjee, but he turns out to be something of a swindler only interested in turning a profit. Rickshaws are hardly all that Grass cracked them up to be anyway, since, as one of the characters points out, someone of presumably lower economic status is required to pedal them.

These thought experiments or 'headbirths' are further intertwined with the story of Hans and Dörte Peters, which he imagines as a new film scenario for Schlöndorff and von Trotta. The Peters are a couple in early middle age who debate whether or not they should bring a child into a dangerous world. They meanwhile take an exotic holiday under the auspices of Sisyphus Tours, which promises an alternative experience for the morally concerned first-world traveller.

Grass as storyteller never tired of inventing new ways to play off narratives against one another in his fiction. Here he reprises a method first tried out in *Local Anaesthetic* where Starusch replays versions of his past on his dentist's television screen. In his next novel, a narrator dreams of a rat who looks back on the atomic apocalypse and recounts a predicted future as if it has already occurred.

The comedy in the Peters' tale was unmistakeable to an audience listening to Grass read but is easy for the reader to miss.[3] They appear at first glance to be Grass's type of people, worried about the state of the world in the same way that he is and for the same reasons, and members of the teaching profession, like his alter ego Hermann Ott, alias Doubt, in *From the Diary of a Snail*. Unlike Grass, the Peters look set to remain childless. One reason is their different take on politics: they are old Sixty-Eighters toying with the idea of switching from the SPD to the Greens. Another is that their existence is unleavened by irony or sensual pleasures, which life continues to offer Grass whatever his view of the contemporary state of politics. *Headbirths* is thus a continuation of his argument with the younger generation begun in *Local Anaesthetic*. It shows a growing interest too in relations with developing-world cultures but questions the leftist notion that the West will benefit from interaction with them as yet another quick-fix solution.

Grass joined the SPD in 1982 in a gesture of solidarity after the FDP withdrew its support for the social–liberal coalition and enabled Helmut Kohl to begin his long term as chancellor, but he had opposed Schmidt on the 'double-track decision'. With the CDU back in office, he took no prisoners in his assessments of the national situation and what should be done, adopting poses which appeared anything but playful. Whereas in the previous decade there had been expansive essays like 'The Worker Who Reads' and 'Kafka and His Legacy', now he engaged exclusively in polemics. He began a month after Kohl formed his first government, with a speech entitled 'The Destruction of Humanity Has Begun'. On 30 January 1983 he addressed the SPD's fiftieth anniversary commemoration of Hitler's accession to power, which was held in Frankfurt's historic Paulskirche, the venue for the first elected German parliament in 1848. The title of his speech: 'On the Right to Resist'; his drift: Germans must make good their failure to prevent Hitler by opposing the calculated escalation in the Cold War. In November 1983, as the Bundestag prepared to debate the proposal to station the new missiles, Grass wrote an emotional letter to all its members which was published in *Die Zeit*, pleading with them to reject the proposal, comparing the historical moment to both 1914 and 1933 and invoking the Germans' responsibility to learn from their past. In May 1985, on the fortieth anniversary of the end of the war, Kohl invited Reagan to pay his respects to the German war dead at the military cemetery at Bitburg, which included more than two dozen ss. This gave Grass an opportunity to reveal his ss secret in another anniversary speech, but he did not take it. Instead, he accused the chancellor of playing fast and loose with history by implying that the Nazis' was a war like any other and its dead deserved honouring in the same way. The Bitburg scandal would have become the Grass ss scandal if he had chosen this moment to reveal his military role in the dying months of the war, and once again he carefully avoided a reference to the ss in his speech. His criticism would be quoted against him in 2006 when he revealed his own brief ss membership, however.

Spokespeople for the new government were sometimes ready to respond to Grass's interventions. Kohl himself called Grass's claim that the Bundeswehr's role in the stationing of new missiles was unconstitutional 'completely absurd and a perfidious calumny of our armed forces'.[4] Unlike Erhard in 1965, Kohl stuck to the issues, knowing that despite the mass demonstrations and blockades of bases public opinion was on his side. His new coalition won the election held in 1983. In May 1984, a clear majority who expressed a view (58 per cent) disagreed with Grass.[5]

Grass's criticism intensified after 9 November 1989 when travel restrictions between East and West Berlin were lifted and the GDR began to crumble. Far from expressing relief that the threat of nuclear destruction was averted and the GDR population could now live in freedom, he saw the West's victory in the Cold War to be the realization of a dual nightmare of a different sort. The forces of the capitalist free market would no longer be held in check and independence for a reunified Germany presented the world with a renewed danger. *The Call of the Toad*, his first post-unification novel, articulates these gloomy predictions and belongs for that reason more closely with *The Rat* and other works from the 1980s than with the major work of reunification, *Too Far Afield*. If we are to periodize Grass's oeuvre across the watershed of 1989–90, then the first work to be published in the new era belongs more to the old than the new.

In the first half of the 1980s, Grass reverted to apocalyptic rhetoric, abandoning pragmatic arguments to depict the world situation in metaphysical or existential terms. Nothing less than the future of civilization – of humanity and life on earth – was at stake. The West was abandoning the Enlightenment by deploying the new missiles. The threat to use them amounted to a plan for genocide on a par with Auschwitz. Writers would have to stick together and speak out for the truth. In December 1981 and March 1983 Grass and his veteran GDR colleague Stephan Hermlin organized writers' conferences, first in East Berlin, then in West Berlin, issuing statements in favour of disarmament on both sides.

Grass campaigned on other global issues, such as poverty in the developing world and environmental pollution. He was moving to the left and now advocated 'democratic socialism' instead of social democracy, though he pleaded for an ideological 'third way' between the two superpowers. He saw this alternative being realized in Nicaragua after the Sandinista Revolution in 1979 and in Poland since the birth of the Solidariność trade union in Gdańsk's shipyards in the hot summer of 1980. While he once teased 'the humorous Enzensberger' for decamping to Cuba in April 1968, in 1982 he himself visited Nicaragua. The principal vehicle for this new politics was the biannual *L76* (relaunched in 1980 as a quarterly under the new title *L80*). *L76* or *L80* was a journal of the pan-European left, conceived as a continuation of the suppressed Czechoslovakian weekly *Literání Listy*, which had been a mouthpiece for the forces of the Prague Spring. *L76* provided an outlet for East

European dissidents, including from the GDR. Many contributors were from Czechoslovakia, such as the former minister in Dubček's government, Zdeněk Mlynář and the playwright Václav Havel, who would become the first post-communist president of the country. Grass remained on the editorial board, continuing to give the journal valuable contributions, and raised funds by auctioning an etching of Heinrich Böll's typewriter. Despite his best efforts, *L80* finally folded in July 1988, sixteen months before the implosion of the Soviet bloc, appropriately enough with an issue dedicated to the memory of the Prague Spring, which was crushed twenty summers ago in August 1968.

It was the nuclear issue which dominated in the first half of the 1980s, however. For anyone who had lived in Berlin through the Cuban Missile Crisis of 1962 (the year the world was predicted to end in *Dog Years* as well as for Father's Day in *The Flounder*), the territory was familiar, but Grass's priorities had changed. In the 1960s he did not question NATO or Adenauer's historic policy of *Westbindung* – or integrating the FRG into the western alliance – or waste his breath decrying the Vietnam War. The West was superior because it allowed free speech and the GDR worthy of comparison with a concentration camp, as he claimed in his open letter to Anna Seghers in August 1961. After *The Plebeians Rehearse the Uprising*, his persistent interventions made him '*the* literary un-person par excellence' for the East Berlin Politburo.[6]

Now he took the fight to New York, speaking at the Book Fair in 1983 and a meeting of PEN in 1985, when he clashed with Saul Bellow, even comparing the situation in the USA under Reagan to that of Germany on the eve of the Nazi takeover. Helen Wolff told him bluntly that he was misreading the American point of view.[7]

His statements were matched by equally dramatic gestures. In August 1986 he and Ute left Germany for Calcutta, ostensibly out of dissatisfaction with the quality of political debate. Grass resigned from the Academy of Arts in 1989 over the withdrawal of an invitation to Salman Rushdie, whom an Islamic cleric had decreed should be killed because of his depiction of religion in a work of fiction, *The Satanic Verses*. In November 1990, in the first post-unification elections and for the first time in his career, Grass did not campaign for the SPD. He resigned from the party in 1992 in a dispute over changes to the asylum laws as expressed in the Grundgesetz.

Grass's understanding of how his literary writing related to his politics was also in a state of flux: both *The Rat* and *The Call of the Toad* were closer in tone and subject-matter to his direct political interventions than any of his earlier fiction. His writing in the 1960s was often directly political too, but whereas *Plebeians* prompted a discussion about the role of progressive writers under 'real existing socialism' and *Local Anaesthetic* anticipated arguments about terrorist violence, Grass was now no longer leading the conversation.

The break from literary writing lasted around three years, until he began work in the summer of 1983 on a project which became *The Rat*, published two and a half years later in March 1986. It is a rather uneven work which did not find favour with reviewers in the same way that *The Flounder* had done. The reception did not stop *The Rat* from topping *Der Spiegel*'s list of best-selling titles for over two months and remaining in the top ten for the rest of 1986. In some ways it has proved more durable than *The Flounder* and was the third of his books to be adapted for the screen, in a television production in 1997.

In German *Rättin* is a made-up word suggesting both 'she-rat' and female advisor (Rätin), from *rat*, meaning counsel or council. Like *The Flounder*, *The Rat* includes poems and interweaves several different narrative threads. It tends to get labelled a 'novel' or *roman*, as it is mainly written in prose and is of the requisite length, though for the first time Grass refused to define the genre of a major work, which is a highly unusual gesture in the world of German publishing.

His suggestion that *The Flounder* be classified as 'a fairy tale' was turned down because it did not sound serious and could adversely affect sales. Grass relented on this occasion but in future would insist on getting his own way on this point. *Too Far Afield* would be the last formal novel he would write: *The Call of the Toad* is another *erzählung*, *Crabwalk* a novella, *My Century* and *Peeling the Onion* have no genre subheadings, while his last two longer prose narratives are classified as 'dark room stories' (*The Box*) and 'a declaration of love' (*Grimms' Words*). By his own counting, the novelist Günter Grass only published four novels, three in his first decade and just one thereafter: *The Tin Drum*, *Dog Years*, *Local Anaesthetic* and *Too Far Afield*. He was in the public mind a *dichter* (poet) rather than a *schriftsteller* (writer), though he preferred the latter term. The public understanding of his vocation was not only determined by the fact that he wrote poems. After joining Steidl publishers at the beginning of the 1990s, his books became more complete works of art with higher production values and a greater prominence for artwork, which Grass always took to be integrated with the printed word rather than an illustration of it. A number of his books appeared in more richly illustrated collector's editions either simultaneously or in advance of print-heavy versions – *My Century*, for instance, and *From Germany to Germany, Diary, 1990*.

He finished *The Rat* in the autumn of 1985 after around two years of writing. He told Figes that 'it marks a clear watershed in my narrative powers. In other words, I have to start taking new risks – and that is what I have always liked doing.'[8] He had expressed a similar feeling that a long creative period had come to an end on finishing *Local Anaesthetic* in 1969. This time it was not until the unexpected tumult of the GDR's collapse that he found new material to ply into a new project in which he really took those risks – *Too Far Afield*. *The Rat* also left him more tired than he remembered being at the end of previous periods of concentrated writing.[9] He was experiencing age-related ailments for the first time, a reminder

After returning from Calcutta, Grass with his dog at the house he and Ute rented on the Baltic island of Møn, 1987.

that he was approaching sixty in October 1987. In July 1987 he submitted to an operation on a troublesome prostate, a condition which also inhibits the now sixty-year-old Oskar Matzerath, whom he resurrects as director of a *Postfuturum* video company in *The Rat*. The novel's celebrated poem 'I Dreamt I Had to Take My Leave', which Helene Grass, who appeared in the television film of the novel, would read at his memorial celebration, is more about intimations of his individual mortality than collective annihilation, though he denied in interviews that this was the case.[10]

Grass could hardly be accused of risk-averseness in *The Rat*. The approach to time and history is fundamentally new. The difference between writing 'fiction against the bomb' as opposed to against a repressive regime is that writers always knew that their words had a good chance of outliving a despotic regime and that their imagining of experience in a work of literature would in time find readers. 'Manuscripts don't burn,' writes Mikhail Bulgakov in *The Master and Margarita*. This is now no longer true.

One of his ideas was to imagine that his whole creative world was coming to an end, but he gave the impression in many quarters that he was running out of material. This is certainly the drift of Günter Ratte in a parody entitled *Der Grass*. Billed as 'a literary prank', this comic inversion of *The Rat* took aim at Grass's perceived pomposity, calling him a court jester who believes he is the king. In *Der Grass*, a rat married to a woman called Tulla dreams that his wish for a poet as a Christmas present is granted (in the first line of Grass's novel, the narrator explains that he wanted a rat for Christmas). The poet is 'Grass', whom the rat keeps in a cage as he listens to his tales about his lifetime achievements, friendships with politicians and gloomy predictions, which the novel's other characters refuse to take seriously: '"We are finished." "You are finished, maybe," said Tulla.'[11]

The idea in Grass's novel that rats will inherit the earth as the only creatures able to survive the human catastrophe is loosely inspired by Douglas Adams's *The Hitchhiker's Guide to the Galaxy*, a British cult sci-fi comedy, which became very popular in Germany.[12] According to Adams, humans were only the third most intelligent species on the planet, after the mice and the dolphins, and it was the mice who commissioned the earth to be made. Grass's rats are similarly pro-active. He would point out that he first wrote about rats in a play from 1958 entitled *Flood*, that they feature too in *Dog Years*, and he develops the idea of 'rattishness' as being one half of a binary opposition in the poem 'Racine Changes His Coat of Arms', which was published in 1960 in *Gleisdreieck*. Once again but arguably for the last time he was returning to his origins for inspiration and unfolding hitherto peripheral ideas and images to their full.

The auto-fictional male voice and his rat partner narrate a number of stories. The artist Lothar Malskat foresees how the world might end and tries to issue a coded warning. But Malskat was convicted of forging medieval frescoes in Lübeck's restored Marienkirche even though he clearly signed them with his own initials. He went to gaol while the real counterfeiters, the twin post-war German villains, Konrad Adenauer in the FRG and Walter Ulbricht in the GDR, carried on with their mutually reinforcing pretences of ideological certainty and thus underpinned national division. The Malskat strand of *The Rat* is based on fact. Vineta, in contrast, is a Baltic Atlantis. Four feminists in the novel peer beneath the waves at the long-lost city of Vineta at the moment the giant explosion puts an end to all life on Earth, only to see that it is already populated by the rats. Grass's vision of this lost underwater world turns out to be Danzig as he last saw it intact in September 1944 when he left for the front. The Baltic Sea was familiar with death and destruction, as Grass reminds readers in his retelling of three ship-sinkings in April 1945 which between them caused thousands of deaths. The Third World War carries on seamlessly from the Second World War, the time in-between being known to the she-rat as 'the inter-war period'.

Grass explained to his editor that the various strands

intensify from chapter to chapter and in the second half of the book they merge with each other and thereby demonstrate the catastrophic outcomes from both narrative perspectives, that of the author and that of the rat.[13]

But the narrative problem with *The Rat* is that the stories have no essential relationship to one another, which was not the case in the many-layered and even over-complicated *The Flounder*, and that the author-narrator consequently switches from one to another as if he is changing television channels. They also all lead in the same direction and none of the figures has any influence over the outcome.

These structural weaknesses must be one of the reasons that Grass found himself on the wrong side of some negative reviews. He was hardly unused to criticism: '*Local Anaesthetic* is getting panned' (v:531), the narrator of *From the Diary of a Snail* comments with a dash of self-deprecating amusement. This time it seemed different though. Grass took the reviews personally, as he tended to do, believing there was a campaign afoot to 'shut [him] up' and that it was to some degree successful.[14] The criticism was also aimed for sure at statements he had made on the state of the world over the previous half a dozen years: he even adapted an open letter to the Bundestag against the missiles in the new novel. From 1986 up to 2012, three years before his death, there would be repeated, seemingly concerted and often privately motivated attempts in the media to reckon with Grass and to discredit his habit of taking a stand. Criticism of *The Rat* was motivated by a refusal to accept his qualifications for making interventions. Nineteen years after the last meeting of Gruppe 47, did Germans still need writers telling them what to do? What could Grass add in this work of fiction to the argument about nuclear rearmament which had not already been said hundreds of times? In the 1960s he campaigned as a novelist who also had something to say about politics; now he risked coming across as a politician who also wrote novels. There was, too, something awry with the novel's timing, since public anxiety on the nuclear issue had peaked by March 1986. Mikhail Gorbachev, the new Soviet leader, was indicating readiness to negotiate disarmament with the USA.

The Rat was followed by another break from writing. This time he also wanted time out from Germany, leaving to live in Calcutta, where he and Ute planned to spend a year. Grass's interest in India, which he first visited in 1975, was not cultural, linguistic or historical, let alone spiritual, as was the case with so many twentieth-century European visitors, but political and in some ways existential. He wanted to confront poverty, to expose himself to degradation and extreme need, which he took to be the flipside of Western prosperity, and to find out how human beings cope when they lack what Westerners take to be necessities.

The literary result was a minor work incorporating ink drawings and two versions of a travelogue, one in verse, the other in prose, which he entitled *Show Your Tongue* after a Hindu gesture denoting shame which is associated with the goddess Kali. Grass feels shame when he sees hunger, want and injustice. In India he looked for reflections of his own interests. He obsessed over national unity versus division and the Enlightenment versus the counter-Enlightenment. Bengal was split in two just like Germany: between the Indian state with Calcutta as its capital and Bangladesh ('free Bengal') with its capital Dakha, which he and Ute also visit. They carried Germany with them in their thoughts and reading bags, which contained weighty works by Schopenhauer and Lichtenberg, representing the two sides of the Enlightenment, and fiction by the Prussian chronicler Theodor Fontane, Ute's favourite writer, as well as a manuscript of *Tallhover* by Hans Joachim Schädlich, a veteran of the East Berlin writers' meetings. The twin ideas for *Too Far Afield* were thus born in Calcutta. Grass was also advising a local production of *The Plebeians Rehearse the Uprising*. The writer Ilija Trojanow calls him 'a travelling menhir',[15] a living monument to his own fame in other words, who does not do what travellers and in particular travel writers are supposed to do: interact with the locals on something approaching their own terms. *Der Spiegel* secretly sent a reporter to shadow him and published a mildly derogatory spoiler for *Show Your Tongue*, though try as the anonymous reporter may have done s/he could not find a Calcutta resident who would say a bad word about their prominent German guests.[16] Once again the book stood in disproportion to the man and the reputation.

Back in Germany, Grass made his first ever reading tours of the GDR, travelling to East Berlin, Leipzig and Dresden in June 1987 and Magdeburg, Erfurt, Halle and Jena in April 1988, this time at the invitation of the Evangelical Church in their series 'Christians Listen to the Voices of Contemporary Artists'.[17] Churches were the only premises in the GDR not under the direct control of the state, which partly explains their prominence in the struggle against the regime. To packed auditoria of up to 1,000 each time, Grass read from *The Rat*, choosing passages relating to the Cold War and the GDR, *The Tin Drum*, which was finally published in the East in 1986, and *Show Your Tongue*. In the Q&A sessions he praised Gorbachev's efforts at *glasnost* and *perestroika* in the USSR, seeing the reforms as a model for other Eastern bloc states, including the GDR, and expressed his belief in the indivisibility of German literature and the unified Germany of culture or *kulturnation*. The date 18 June 1988 found him in Petzow am Schwielowsee just outside Potsdam assisting the chairman of the West German Writers' Association, Anna Jonas, at a meeting with her East German counterpart, Hermann Kant, and his Stasi minder. The Westerners vainly argued for a joint declaration in favour of disarmament on both sides. Grass spoke up for the rehabilitation of Erich Loest, who had spent seven years in Bautzen in the 1950s, also to no effect.[18] In June 1989, this time at the invitation of the culture association (Kulturbund), for which Fonty in *Too Far Afield* would give many a lecture, Grass read on the Baltic islands of Hiddensee, Ute's birthplace, and Rügen, where Philipp Otto Runge in *The Flounder* claimed to have heard the tale of 'The Fisherman and His Wife'. He then travelled south to the Erzgebirge to sketch trees stricken by acid rain for his next publication, *Dead Wood*. The Stasi kept a close watch as always, tailing him in the streets, planning his likely movements and collecting reports on his activities.

Then came the news on the evening on 9 November 1989 that the Berlin Wall was opened, which set in train a series of events which sealed the end of the communist German state. From late 1989, Grass was at the centre of media attention, this time as the major voice of opposition, first to the very idea that Germany should unify, preferring a confederation of two states as he had argued consistently for 25 years, then to the manner in which the Kohl government handled the unification process.[19] Grass was wrong on the first point, as he was in time forced to concede, but arguably right on the second, as developments to this day continue to demonstrate and he maintained to the very end.

Over the following nine to ten months, Grass was busier than at any point in his life. He gave a major interview in *Der Spiegel* immediately after the fall of the Wall before it was possible to predict the course which events would take.[20] He was prepared for this turn of events and had a plan. What was needed first of all was what he called 'burden equalizing', a massive transfer of funds from West to East to ensure the survival of a reformed GDR under new leadership, which Grass saw as historical compensation for the GDR having suffered the consequences of defeat in 1945 on behalf of all Germans.[21] In January 1990 he rushed out a paperback containing material on the national question: articles, interviews and poems which he had published since the early 1960s.[22] He wanted to show that he had been on the case since 1961 and that his anti-communist credentials were impeccable. In February there were two major articles in *Die Zeit*, the second his long-awaited Frankfurt Lecture on poetics which he now gave the programmatic title 'Writing after Auschwitz'.[23] Each was hurriedly reissued in pamphlet form. He gave interviews on radio and television, including with *Spiegel* editor Rudolf Augstein, and travelled through the still existing GDR, reading from his works and, up to the first free elections of 18 March 1990, talking, cajoling and organizing.

In the run-up to these elections, which were held coincidentally on the anniversary of the 1848 Revolution, he argued with voters to reject the march to unification and to safeguard the continued existence of a separate GDR state. A letter to the leader of the newly founded GDR branch of the SPD, Ibrahim Böhme, gives some indications of how Grass misunderstood the forces driving this revolution. He wants to revive the spirit of his '65 and '69 campaigns in the FRG, offering performances with percussionist Günter 'Baby' Sommer of a routine they called 'There Once Was a Country' and public discussions with local SPD candidates of *The Plebeians Rehearse the Uprising.* The second half of the letter concerns Erich Loest, who has joined the SPD and is prepared to speak at the next party conference. Grass compares him with Havel, who was soon to be elected president of Czechoslovakia, and closes his letter with the wish that GDR social democrats should – despite all the pressures – rediscover their 'distinctive GDR sense of humour'.[24] The problem with Grass's strategy was that Böhme was no Brandt. The SPD crashed at the election, polling just 22 per cent compared with almost 50 per cent for the 'Alliance for Germany', the main component of which was the East German CDU, one of the 'block parties' permitted in the GDR to simulate democratic representation for the middle class. Shortly afterwards Böhme was outed as a Stasi stooge. Ibrahim was an adopted name: he was not Jewish, though he liked people to assume that he was.

Loest, on the other hand, could only have made an East German Havel if his compatriots had backed their intelligentsia and shared their wish to reform along socialist lines. But this is the path they rejected when they switched from chanting '*wir sind das Volk*' to '*wir sind ein Volk*' (we are the people; we are a single people). Many GDR dissidents whom Grass knew well (Schädlich was a major exception) differed from their counterparts in other Soviet-bloc states in their wish to reform the political system rather than do away with it. Christa Wolf, Christoph Hein, Heiner Müller and Stefan Heym addressed an estimated three-quarters of a million demonstrators on 4 November 1989, all essentially arguing this case. They undoubtedly spoke to a constituency but the mass of the population had other ideas and Western capital was not slow to take advantage. Grass was fascinated by how this happened. The main character in *Too Far Afield*, Theo Wuttke, alias 'Fonty' because of his passion for Fontane, speaks at the rally on 4 November. Reschke and Piątkowska in *The Call of the Toad* have been compared to the East German activists of the first hour who were swiftly pushed aside by a combination of market forces and the promise of prosperity.[25]

Two weeks after his letter to Böhme, Grass took part in a televised debate with *Der Spiegel* editor Rudolf Augstein, which he was judged to have lost badly. Augstein rounded on him, saying that his argument that because of the Holocaust Germans did not deserve to reunify, amounted to 'religion' rather than politics.[26]

After the March election, Grass shifted his position and found himself on somewhat firmer ground criticizing the way reunification was being handled. In his eyes what was happening was the annexation of the smaller state by the larger rather than the merger of two equals (he used the loaded term *Anschluß*, or annexation, which the Nazis deployed for their takeover of Austria in 1938). He took the whole process to be against not just the spirit but the very letter of the Grundgesetz, which was originally intended as an interim document which should now be superseded by a constitution elaborated in consultation with all Germans. Grass insisted that he was right on this point to the end of his life.

There was much to criticize in the way that the West went about unification. Jobs were destroyed as state-owned enterprises were closed down by the Treuhand agency, which was set up to look for buyers for the GDR's industries. Unemployment rose rapidly. Professionals were 'evaluated' and often removed from their posts because of past compromises with the regime. Life experiences counted for nothing. When the 'blossoming landscapes' promised by Kohl failed to materialize, disappointment set in. Rural areas and small towns suffered population loss as the young headed west in search of opportunities. For these reasons the successor party to the SED, which ruled the GDR for forty years, retains a significant presence in the regional state parliaments and gained more than fifty seats in the Bundestag in 2017. The populist movements which cluster around the Alternative für Deutschland party and Pegida organization also have their power base in the eastern states of Saxony and Thuringia.

Grass's series of interventions fed directly into *The Call of the Toad*, his first post-unification work, the narrative of which spans the events of reunification from November 1989 to June 1991. He concentrates on post-Wall Gdańsk and German-Polish relations rather than Germany itself, and combines satire on German expellee associations and their functionaries with a critique of free-market capitalism, which now ruled unchallenged across the old Soviet bloc. His theme was typically macabre. He explained to Wolff, to whom the book would be dedicated, that he was interested in how former Danzigers were exploiting the catastrophic situation to buy up cemeteries in Gdańsk and backing up their wish to be buried in the soil of their *Heimat* or homeland with hard currency.[27] *The Call of the Toad* is his only work of fiction to be the subject of an extended meta-commentary in the form of *From Germany to Germany*: *Diary, 1990*, where he reveals that he originally entertained the idea of publishing it in the same volume as two of his anti-unification speeches. The work of fiction itself has now become for Grass an intervention, meant to provoke reactions in the same way as a speech or newspaper article, which are themselves pieces of semi-literary rhetoric often taking him weeks to craft.

According to the central narrative conceit in *The Call of the Toad*, a nameless narrator, who bears some resemblance to Grass himself, receives a bundle of documents from the deceased principal characters, his old Danzig school chum Alexander Reschke and his new Polish wife Alexandra Piątkowska, which he is asked to fashion into a narrative. He does this in real time, so to speak, as *The Call of the Toad* was published in May 1992, just eleven months after the fictional protagonists' deaths in a car crash in southern Italy.

Time takes a number of other forms in this new work. The second day of November, when it begins, is All Souls' Day, when Catholics remember the dead who have not been accepted into heaven. Their stories have not yet reached their end and they haunt the living as uncompleted beings. Piątkowska intends to visit the grave of her parents, but the eternal peace of their souls is less on her mind than the thought that they would have preferred to lie somewhere else, namely their home city of Vilnius. As far as their daughter is concerned, if she could correct this situation, order in the world would be restored. This idea gathers legs, so to speak, because on account of all the expulsions after the Second World War, many people are not buried where they would like to be.

In German folk mythology a toad's croaking signals a disaster on the horizon. According to the narrator, a number of Romantic poets, including Clemens Brentano and Achim von Arnim, cite this myth.[28] There is also 'A Fairy Tale about the Toad' in the Grimm brothers' collection of *Children's and Household Tales*. Thus whereas 'The Call of the Toad' has no immediate meaning in English, the original from which this phrase is translated, *Unkenrufe*, has a ready sense of Cassandra-like doom-mongering in German. A number of toads play an intra-diegetic function in the story: they lollop into view on the edge of roads, where they are in danger of getting flattened, or make themselves heard at unpropitious moments. Reschke is nicknamed 'the toad' because of his often pessimistic outlook, which is allied to an ability to predict the future and reflect on the present from that vantage point.

Nothing turns out the way it was supposed to in *The Call of the Toad*. The two lovers retreat into their private happiness by getting married. In time-honoured German fashion, they take a honeymoon in Italy, where Piątkowska has never visited. After most probably getting to Naples, they are killed when their car swerves off a deserted coastal road.

There were two other literary manifestations of Grass's toadish warnings: a volume of drawings and short texts on the cross-border problem of the dying forests, *Dead Wood*, and a collection of thirteen sonnets, *Novemberland*. The culprit in *Dead Wood* was acid rain from industrial plants on both sides of the former Iron Curtain. Here

Grass was shortly overtaken by events: acid rain soon ceased to be a problem as the factories either closed or fitted effective filters and the forests quickly recovered. Some of the symbolism of *The Call of the Toad* is reworked in *Novemberland*. Grass's fourth sonnet bears the title 'All Souls', which ends more pessimistically than the novel: 'All hope was in vain: / On All Souls Day all the graves are open' (1:288). November is symbolically the lowest point in the national calendar, associated with oppression and censorship. Since Heinrich Heine's *Germany: A Winter's Tale*, poets and politicians have invoked this imagery. Heine begins with the lines:

It was in the glum month of November,
With days growing overcast,
And the wind tearing leaves from the trees,
When I left for Germany at last.

The symbolism was potent in 1977 when the showdown between the state and the RAF became known as the German Autumn. Since the days of Heine, Germans had experienced the November Revolution of 1918, Hitler's Beer Hall Putsch in 1923 and the Kristallnacht in 1938, all of which took place on the ninth day of the eleventh month, the same day that the Berlin Wall came down in 1989.

Events over the next year or so in Germany, including attacks on asylum seekers and immigrants, seemed to bear out Grass's pessimism. In September 1992, in the face of growing right-wing extremism and the burning down of an asylum-seekers' hostel in Rostock, Grass was moved to write of 'Weimar conditions', apparently the first time that he had ever used that phrase.[29] In November that year he gave a major speech with the title 'Speech on Loss', on the dire state of the nation.

In an emotional outburst on the eve of unification, Grass had written to Egon Bahr, what they are going to call Germany on 3 October is no longer my state. – Well, you can live without a state; Germany will still exist as a country and the German language will not have been taken from me.[30]

This position on Kohl's new Germany echoed Kurt Tucholsky's rejection of the Weimar Republic in 1926, which Grass condemned in 1968 (XI:389). He could hardly sustain it for long now. Fittingly for a writer who was a novelist first and a politician second, he worked through his change of feeling in a work of fiction, the novel *Too Far Afield*.

6

Learning to Love the Berlin Republic: *Too Far Afield*

In a fragment from 1797, Goethe and Schiller discuss the dramatic genre as dealing with events which are 'completely present' while the epic deals with 'the completely past'.[1] If there is still validity in their distinction, it would help explain why Grass gave up writing plays with the stage version of *Local Anaesthetic* in 1969, which he entitled, oxymoronically following Goethe and Schiller, *Before*. When it comes to prose, Grass would also not have pleased the arbiters of classical taste. Whatever prose genre he practises (novel, novella, *erzählung* or memoir), the past can never be completely over. History is always with him, which is why he sees the present in the past and depicts current events as palimpsests showing traces of multiple histories. He is interested in the connections between different layers of time which interact dynamically with each other. In the fiction of the first decade, this meant that he saw how the horrific experiences of the Third Reich still invaded the consciousness of his characters, even if they suppressed their memories of them, and the consequences of their deeds and omissions remained in their minds. In *The Flounder* he encompassed all human history in the quintessentially German crucible of his home city; in *The Rat* he imagined the end of all time as having both already happened and not happened yet.

Now, in *Too Far Afield*, he presents the twentieth-century life of Theo Wuttke (born 1919), alias 'Fonty', through the life and writings of Theodor Fontane (1819–1898), who is Fonty's all-consuming obsession. Fonty has lived through the Third Reich and the war, during which he saw service in Poland and was stationed in occupied France, and experienced the entire forty-year history of the GDR, during which he worked as a lecturer for the Kulturbund and, following demotion for unwanted political comments, as a humble messenger in the GDR 'house of ministries'. This is one of the key locations and *lieux de mémoire* in the novel, as it was previously the headquarters of the Luftwaffe and from 1990 housed the controversial Treuhand agency tasked with disposing of state-owned GDR enterprises. In wartime France Fonty got caught up with the resistance; during the invasion of Poland he wrote reports for the Gestapo. In the GDR he collaborated with the Stasi in the shape of the mild-mannered though decidedly sinister Ludwig Hoftaller, his 'day-and-night shadow' who both blackmails and looks after him and his family, even nursing them during a shared spell of bad health. Fonty is above all a free and critical spirit, repeatedly in trouble for his unorthodox views, which he expresses through coded allusions to Fontane, but, though never a member of the party, firmly wedded to the idea of a 'workers' and peasants' state'. He is a much humbler version of critical writers Grass knew well, such as Christa Wolf, Stefan Heym and Heiner Müller, alongside whom Fonty addresses the famous rally on 4 November 1989 at Berlin's Alexanderplatz. In the course of twenty months which are charted in the novel's 700 pages, which make *Too Far Afield* Grass's longest work of prose fiction, Fonty gradually disinvests his emotions from the GDR and learns to take advantage of new opportunities.

Theodor Fontane was compromised to a similar degree and critical of Prussia in the Bismarckian and immediate post-Bismarckian eras. He drew on an even richer source of experience, having first lived through the Metternich system of police control in the so-called *Vormärz* – the period from roughly 1830 to the political upheavals in numerous European capitals which began in March 1848 – taken part half-heartedly in the 1848 revolution (though tending more towards the conservatives than the democrats), and then reported for the Prussian government on political exiles in London while earning money from opportunistic newspaper articles. Only in middle age did he begin to write books, first popular accounts of Bismarck's 'wars of unification' (against Denmark, Austria and France) as well as ballads and finally the novels which truly made his name and count as the finest examples of social realism in the German language. Fontane loved an idea of Prussia which he increasingly located in the past while pillorying the mercantile ethos of the *Gründerzeit* (in *Frau Jenny Treibel*) after the first unification of Germany in 1870, the notion of honour (in *Effi Briest*) and class-bound behaviour in choosing marital partners (*Trials and Tribulations*).

As Fonty knows every word written by his 'one and only', he reacts to the sudden upheaval of 1989–91 by referring constantly to events and characters in Fontane's life and oeuvre. He compares and asks questions, though in an essentially unsystematic way, treating the previous unification of 1870–71 and repression under Metternich pre-1848 or under Bismarck's Socialist Laws post-1878 as if they are contemporary events or at least have a direct bearing on the present. The historical purview of *Too Far Afield* thus extends from 1819, the year both of Fontane's birth and Metternich's Carlsbad Decrees, through to October 1991. If this is largely new territory in his fiction, Grass's speeches are peppered with references to modern German history. He argued in 1971, for instance, on the centenary of the first unification of Germany, that the defeated liberal forces of 1848 came to the fore a hundred years later with the founding of the FRG and finally took over the reins of power when Brandt became chancellor in 1969.[2] This is part of the long battle for hegemony which Grass now chronicles.

Too Far Afield represents a turning point in Grass's thinking on the national question, however. When Fonty disappears into the Cévennes at the end of the novel in the company of his rediscovered

French granddaughter, Madeleine Aubron, he is enacting a personal form of *Westbindung* which, while the policy of the federal government since 1949, had not shaped Grass's understanding of Germany hitherto. This was reflected in the shape and trajectory of his novel narratives: Oskar, too, fled to France at the end of *The Tin Drum* but was arrested and brought back to Germany, while both *The Flounder* and *The Rat* ended in Gdańsk.

The new novel's concealed theme is liberation. Fonty's co-dependent relationship with Hoftaller makes him neither happy nor fulfilled. While he is unimpressed by the ideology of profit and money-making which he encounters in the West, the novel is structured around his repeated attempts to escape Germany. In the end Hoftaller's blackmail threats are revealed as empty and Fonty effects his escape. In symbolic terms his reconciliation with Madeleine, the result of a secret wartime affair which gave Hoftaller ammunition for his blackmail, entails redemption from the long nightmare of German national history.

Grass borrows the character Hoftaller from Schädlich's novel *Tallhover*, which he first read in Calcutta in 1986. Tallhover is a seemingly immortal secret policeman who serves every regime from the 1840s to the early 1950s, when, to Grass's disappointment, Schädlich kills him off.[3] In early 1991, as he was starting *The Call of the Toad*, he had already approached Schädlich for permission to give Tallhover a new lease of life. Grass's secret policeman is a very different individual from Schädlich's, however. Tallhover is an unpleasant man with no redeeming features who carries out his orders without reflection, while Hoftaller is essentially harmless.

According to *Diary, 1990*, Grass was already researching *Too Far Afield*, which he initially called *Treuhand*, when he began *The Call of the Toad*.[4] He set to work immediately on the next project before *The Call of the Toad* was even published, going over the same time span for a second time (*Too Far Afield* starts on Fonty's seventieth birthday on 30 December 1989 and ends in September 1991; *The Call of the Toad* begins equally precisely on 2 November 1989 and ends in June 1991). Grass had worked this way only once before, all of thirty years ago when he corrected some of the exuberance of *The Tin Drum* in the more sober *Dog Years*. Now the correction is thematic rather than methodological. Reschke and Piątkowska escape by travelling to Italy, where they are killed. Fonty and Hoftaller are under fewer illusions about what the future holds, but when Fonty escapes to France he has the prospect of a fulfilled old age. For the first time Grass employed a researcher (the literary scholar Dieter Stolz, whose PhD on his use of imagery Grass admired) to gather information on locations and contemporary or historical figures, after discovering that it was impossible for him to visit a venue such as the Treuhand building without being recognized and chaperoned to the PR department.[5] For *My Century* and *Crabwalk*, the historian Olaf Mischler played a similar role.

Another connection with *The Call of the Toad* is the use made of an archive, either the Fontane papers in Potsdam or the bundle of documents connected with the German-Polish cemetery society. In both novels, archivist narrators piece together the truth about a pair of lives from disparate sources and witness statements. *Too Far Afield* is narrated by a small team of self-styled 'footnote slaves' from the Fontane Archive who go out into the field to observe the object of their enquiries as he goes about his business. The purpose of their collectively produced novel is to find an explanation for Fonty's disappearance.

Grass adapts the titles of both novels from the same stanza of an epic poem by Niklaus Lenau about the crushing of the Albigensian heresy in the thirteenth century, which was published in 1843. The stanza in question describes 'the wide battlefield' when 'the toad croak of doubt' over the purpose of so much slaughter can be heard once the fighting is over.[6] Why did he not draw attention to this key allusion in a novel which teems with advertised intertextual references to Fontane's works? Educated German readers recognize '*ein weites Feld*' (a wide field) as a quotation from the last line of Fontane's adultery novel *Effi Briest* when the father of the ill-fated child bride refuses to confront his and his wife's complicity in their disgraced daughter's early death by simply asserting that it is just too broad a topic (too 'wide a field') to contemplate. It is as well known in Germany as any line of Shakespeare in the English-speaking world. According to Stolz, Grass gives the slightest of clues: Ezekiel is the name of a dachshund which makes the briefest of appearances and is also the book in the Old Testament to which Lenau's poem also alludes.[7] Is Grass toying with his readers, challenging us to pick up clues in a trail and not to settle for the most obvious conclusions? He would hardly be the first modernist author to adopt such a tactic. In autobiographical texts he plays cat and mouse with past and future biographers in a similar way. *Too Far Afield* is not obscure in other ways, however, as can seem the case to readers put off by the discussion of Fontane's busy life and copious writings. The references quickly become self-explanatory. The novel's Danish translator Per Øhrgaard initially assumed he would need copious footnotes in his version but erased them one by one as each became redundant.

Similarities with *The Call of the Toad* aside, the new novel represents a fresh departure in most respects: it is set in and around Berlin and has nothing at all to do with Danzig/Gdańsk; and the unidentified narrators, one of whom is female, are not auto-fictional or authorial ciphers of any sort. *Too Far Afield* has no animal motifs, no grotesque or fantastic metaphors, no poems or other interruptions to the narrative flow, which is richly allegorical but stylistically realist. Coming eighteen years after *The Flounder*, the same gap which separated *The Flounder* from *The Tin Drum*, it does not herald a series of works similar in scope or subject-matter. The only subsequent work which it remotely resembles is *Grimms' Words*, which juxtaposes the mid-nineteenth-century lives of Jacob and Wilhelm Grimm with Grass's own campaign exploits in the 1960s and 1970s.

The imaginative run-up to writing *Too Far Afield* was also uniquely brief. While flounders and rats already feature in Grass's imagination before he published *The Tin Drum*, the first indication that Fontane would become a presence in his creative world occurs in 1986. The chapter for that year in *My Century* retells his dream of Ute consorting with Fontane, whose books she has taken with her to Calcutta, and Grass imagining that he must henceforth share his wife with the novelist. *Too Far Afield* is dedicated to Ute 'who has a thing about F'. This is not to say that the celebrated Prussian chronicler of Huguenot stock was not well known to Grass up to this point. Fontane's last novel *Der Stechlin* is listed in Grass's 'The Worker Who Reads' essay as the first novel in German to depict an election;[8] *Effi Briest* even had a place in his mother's bookcase, appropriately enough given that it includes a memorable description of Cassubians.

Fontane enjoyed something of a boom once West Germans discovered remnants of historic Prussia on their doorstep now that they too enjoyed the freedom to travel. Copies of his multi-volume *Wanderings through Brandenburg* were suddenly piled high in Berlin bookshops. F. C. Delius (*The Pear Trees of Ribbeck*, 1991) and Rolf Hochhuth (*Effi's Night*, 1996) both reimagined classic Fontane texts. No other West German author except Grass could have written an epic novel set in the dying GDR, however. Many Eastern readers welcomed the focus on their experience. For details of how people lived, how they spoke, dressed and pursued careers, what they ate and drank, what songs they sang, what they did in their spare time, where they went on holiday and what they wanted for their children, Grass drew on his visits to writers' flats and houses in East Berlin in the mid-1970s, his many friendships with GDR writers, and his own opportunities to speak to readers during his late reading tours in 1987 and 1988.

Ute was a former refugee from East Germany, having grown up on a Baltic island, as was Ingrid Krüger, a native of Erfurt, who was responsible for GDR writers at Luchterhand at the time of her affair with Grass. *Too Far Afield* is nevertheless a Western writer's take on Eastern history.

It was one of the first imaginative treatments in fiction of the Wende period, or 'time of change' as 1989–90 quickly came to be known. Other authors and film-makers have taken very different approaches. The most famous depictions are probably films such as *Goodbye, Lenin!* (dir. Wolfgang Becker, 2003), the Oscar-winning *The Lives of Others* (dir. Florian Henckel von Donnersmarck, 2006) and *Barbara* (dir. Christian Petzold, 2012), which are either feel-good fairy tales or redemptive accounts of resistance heroics. Major fictional accounts tend to be written from the point of view of marginalized or counter-culture characters. This is indicated already in some of the titles: *While We Were Dreaming* (Clemens Meyer, 2006), *The Tower* (Uwe Tellkamp, 2008) and *Kruso* (Lutz Seiler, 2014). Thomas Brussig's *Heroes Like Us*, a best-seller which appeared the same year as *Too Far Afield*, is a picaresque, semi-fantastic account of the narrator's youth which stands in the modern tradition of *The Tin Drum*. Disaffection and naive credulity are the basic themes in this whole body of literature. Seiler's *Kruso*, which won the German Book Prize in 2014, is about passive resistance on the idyllic island of Hiddensee and brave attempts to escape across the sea to Scandinavia. Politically, it recalls Alfred Andersch's *Sansibar, or The Last Reason* (1957), which also centres on an escape across the Baltic and where, as Grass made a point of criticizing, the Nazis are known as 'the others'.[9]

On publication on 28 August 1995 *Too Far Afield* became headline news and remained so for several weeks. Savage reviews were printed in *Der Spiegel*, *Die Zeit* and the *Frankfurter Allgemeine Zeitung*. Reich-Ranicki denounced the novel as a useless piece of writing in front of an audience of several million on national television. The invectives can be understood in part as delayed responses to Grass's one-man campaign against unification, his initial insistence that Germans no longer had the right to nation statehood and his assumption that the GDR, or at the very least the internal opposition to it, retained a degree of legitimacy. Øhrgaard compares the novel's reception with that of Mann's *Doctor Faustus* in 1947: neither work was patriotic enough.[10] This was now indeed a political and to some extent too a generational argument, arguably the biggest of Grass's career. It was caused above all by his dual public role, as it was the politician behind the novel who was being judged. He was now setting out to explore politically charged ideas and events in a work of fiction claiming all the usual freedoms of a novelist. Yet, contrary to what most reviewers assumed, *Too Far Afield* ultimately welcomes unification and inscribes 1991, when the action ends, as the end date of a period of authoritarian history which began in 1819 with the infamous Carlsbad Decrees. Fifty years after the end of the war, Grass himself was making his own peace with a 'normalized' Germany.

'The Fonty Case' was a battle about reputation and the access to the public sphere which Grass's reputation gave him.[11] It was not only about him and his novel. Writers and intellectuals in both German states had enjoyed status and prestige. In the West they had a moral authority which they used to advise their compatriots, none more so than Grass. In the East, writers critical of the state, such as Wolf, Heym and Müller, did not want to do away with the GDR; after the Wende they suddenly looked like loyal supporters rather than dissidents. The West German media first picked a fight with Christa Wolf in the summer of 1990 when she published *What Remains* about her experiences of Stasi observation and harassment in the late 1970s. The criticism was that she had not been brave enough to publish it at the time, as she could have done in the West, and that she was now presenting herself as a victim. Wolf had also briefly co-operated with the Stasi at the beginning of her career and written a novel which she later disowned. At this point it was harder to discredit Grass, but his critics could now pore over his big novel in an attempt to do so.

One of the main motivations in writing *Too Far Afield* was 'to disturb the victors over their breakfast', as he put it, by writing from the point of view of the defeated, even from that of members of the dreaded Stasi.[12] This was part of a battle over how the GDR should be discussed and remembered: the Stasi's worst actions were used by the West German media and politicians to discredit the whole population and in particular writers and intellectuals who may at one or another point in their lives have co-operated with it. Nobody suffered more in this regard than Wolf. At a memorial celebration in 2011 at the Akademie der Künste in Berlin, Grass accused the journalists Ulrich Greiner and Frank Schirrmacher of maligning a great German writer.[13] He and Wolf became friends and began writing to each other in the summer of 1990.

There were many reasons that 'the Fonty case' took the form it did: tearing a novel by the country's leading writer to shreds made good theatre, especially on TV; and there were scores to settle, not least between Grass and Reich-Ranicki. But the dismissal of *Too Far Afield* on the grounds of its lack of literary quality does not wash. As well as stating that it was long-winded, badly written and a crass vehicle for ill-informed opinion, his critics found at least one element in the plot and three remarks by characters to be politically beyond the pale. These are substantive criticisms which are worth investigating. The plot element concerns the assassination of the head of the Treuhand, known in the novel as 'the Boss' and based on Detlev Karsten Rohwedder, who was killed in his living room by a professional marksman firing from a distance of some 40 metres on 1 April 1991. No one was ever charged with this murder, which was claimed by the Red Army Faction, though speculation was widespread that former Stasi elements were involved. There is even a conspiracy theory that Rohwedder was killed by the state because he was about to publish alternative proposals for ex-GDR industries.[14] Grass's Boss is a sympathetic man who is distinctly uneasy at the role of winding up former state enterprises. This corresponds with the known facts about Rohwedder's personality and politics: he was an SPD member who did not want to be an instrument of neo-liberalism. Fonty, comparing as always the evidence before his own eyes with Fontane's writings, identifies the most likely culprit to be working as a cleaner in the Treuhand building, seeing her as a contemporary incarnation of the heroine of Fontane's unfinished novel *Mathilde Möhring*. Her motivation is that her husband has been made redundant. Given that the Rohwedder assassination was carried out by professionals using a sophisticated rifle, it is hardly likely that such a worker could have been responsible, but that is not the point. Grass does not express an apologia for the killers but presents the killing as a tragedy, showing understanding for both the Boss and the victims of the policies the Treuhand was enacting.

One of the remarks which caused offence also concerns terrorism. Fonty says of the German chancellor, who is known throughout the novel as 'the governing mass' (*die regierende Masse*), that 'people like him never took a hit' (*seinesgleichen war nie zu treffen*). This suggests that Fonty may wish the opposite to be the case, but 'hit' can be taken metaphorically. The same is true also of the phrase 'comfortable dictatorship' (*kommode Diktatur*) which Fonty uses to downplay the GDR's repressive character. Grass points out that the phrase is a quotation from a letter by Fontane himself in which he is complaining about Bismarckian Prussia.[15] But he does support Fonty's comment applied to the GDR, arguing elsewhere that by the standards set by twentieth-century dictatorships the GDR dictatorship was indeed 'comfortable', levels of violence and repression being worse under some regimes supported by the West, such as Greece under the colonels or Pinochet's Chile. As he visited Greece in March 1972 and spoke out determinedly against it, just as he supported dissidents in the GDR and visited them, Grass had some idea of what he was talking about.[16]

The final detail in the novel which critics decried was Hoftaller's suggestion that the Stasi made the decision to allow free travel between East and West Berlin, which was announced on the evening of 9 November 1989 by a rather bemused Politburo member, Günter Schabowski, reading from a piece of paper passed to him by an unseen hand. This claim is not endorsed by the novel as it sounds like an empty boast. Yet its veracity cannot be completely ruled out and more than a quarter of a century after the announcement we are still no closer to finding out who wrote the note and how it got passed to Schabowksi. After the Rohwedder assassination, it is the other great mystery of the Wende.

A reader whose objections do have to be taken seriously was Schädlich, the author of the novel from which Grass adapted his second most important character. He was a colleague from the mid-1970s meetings in East Berlin whose first suppressed work, *Attempted Proximity*, Grass championed in 1977. Grass designed the cover and read extracts from it on his national tour promoting *The Flounder*. The rift between the two men caused by *Too Far Afield* lasted for the rest of Grass's life, attempts by Grass's office to affect a reconciliation being rebuffed by Schädlich. As with Reich-Ranicki, the contention is that Grass has appropriated history, whether Jewish or East German, which does not belong to him. In contrast to Reich-Ranicki, who largely limited himself to dramatic criticisms of novels which he found irritating, Schädlich, ever the systematic rhetorician, laid out his objections precisely.

Grass could have expected such a clash, but it apparently took him by surprise that his colleague was not interested in sharing a reading platform (and thereby making some money from book sales) when Grass toured to read from *Too Far Afield*. In the early 1990s the two authors took opposite sides in the debate over what to do with the Stasi files. Grass did not agree that the files should be opened to the public: first, because the reports were inaccurate and contradictory, and second, finding out which of your friends or colleagues was allegedly spying on you would only generate resentment and encourage recriminations. Schädlich favoured openness and even edited a paperback collection of essays by prominent former dissidents, including the future federal president Joachim Gauck, about their Stasi experiences, and how their lives are documented in their files.[17]

Schädlich did approve, however, Grass's use of *Tallhover* in early 1991. The occasion was a brief conversation overheard by others after a dinner at the German Embassy in Rome – which sounds eerily reminiscent of how Reich-Ranicki gave permission for use of an episode from his survival in Nazi-occupied Warsaw in a future work. In pre-publication correspondence four years later, extracts from which Schädlich published without consulting Grass, he objected to the depiction of the GDR and unification, the friendly relationship between Hoftaller and Fonty, and in particular to the suggestion at the end of the novel that Hoftaller will now find work with either the secret services in unified Germany or the CIA. Schädlich accepted that all states use similar methods of surveillance but not that they made similar use of the information they thus obtained, which is rightly or wrongly how he interpreted Grass's standpoint.

Their dispute overlapped with a different controversy over the merging of the West and East German PEN Associations. While Grass was in favour, Schädlich, along with at least two other former participants at the East Berlin meetings in the 1970s, Günter Kunert and Sarah Kirsch, was opposed as long as East German PEN allowed membership to colleagues with Stasi connections.[18] This argument between those former GDR citizens who saw no good in the state in which they once lived and those whose view was more nuanced would rumble on for most of the rest of Grass's life. Grass remained loyal to his chosen side. While he worked closely with Daniela

Dahn, he was criticized by Monika Maron on the publication of his *Diary, 1990* in 2009 when she accused him of the very crime he himself levelled against other Westerners because, in her view, he was telling the *ossis*, or former easteners, what to think and what to want: 'He is the colonizer, if only in spirit.'[19] The battle lines were distinctly fuzzy: Maron had once made an arrangement with the Stasi, which included supplying them with information on her Western contacts, for which in turn Schädlich could not forgive her.[20]

Grass could not have known in 1995 that Schädlich's family had an even more disturbing link with the Stasi than that presented in either his or Schädlich's work of fiction. Schädlich already knew, however, that his brother Karl-Heinz had been closely involved with them under the code name Schäfer (Shepherd) and had reported on the East Berlin meetings, pretending even that he had been invited to attend one, though this did not become public until more than a decade later.[21]

Too Far Afield is another episodic novel – even some of its fiercest reviewers admitted to having favourite chapters or sequences. Reich-Ranicki singled out the vision of Uwe Johnson who appears to the two main figures in Fontane's birthplace, Neuruppin. Others preferred the wedding of Fonty's daughter Martha to the Western businessman which is presided over by a clergyman who preaches doubt. The novel was welcomed by Fontane scholars and has gained in critical reputation since publication, but it has not yet stepped out of the shadow of the ideological arguments with which it was entangled from its inception. Grass would avoid contentious subject-matter and concentrate on shorter forms and autobiography from now on.

7

The New Nation Is Me

In 1994, another election year which saw Kohl once again confirmed as chancellor, Grass told an SPD party manager that 'I am against the Germans doing without an enlightened national consciousness.'[1] He meant not just his old idea of a German *kulturnation* but a sense of themselves in a single nation state. Four years later, in the run-up to only the second election in post-war history which resulted in a new head of government, Grass sent the SPD leader Gerhard Schröder the draft of a speech on 'The Nation and Europe'. Schröder grappled with the same question during his seven years at the head of the first red–green (SPD–Green Party) coalition. Grass's thoughts now echoed those of the influential historian Heinrich August Winkler, who argued that the point of the supranational European Union was to give the nations a space in which they could express themselves nationally but in a peaceable and non-antagonistic way. Winkler's magnum opus, *Germany: The Long Road to the West*, appeared in 2000.[2] In 1998 Grass wanted Germany to enter 'a united Europe as a "mature" nation':

> A united Europe must not develop into a mere economic alliance. The nations with their specific cultural characteristics will carry on existing within it. For us Germans this depends on us finally conceiving of ourselves as a nation without any nationalistic subtext.[3]

He continued to argue for a new constitution to replace the old Grundgesetz, but he could not persuade the new government to revisit that old proposal. The problem for Grass was that, for as long as this did not happen, instead of a newly defined nation state, what emerged was an enlarged version of the old Federal Republic. Most Germans seemed quite content to live with that, however, including the *ossis*.

There are no other big new causes after 1990 and fewer high-profile public lectures than in previous decades. His interventions were aligned with the SPD once again, which the CDU-led government up to 1998 certainly noticed. When Grass took the opportunity in October 1997 of criticizing Kohl's decision to take Turkish Kurds off the list of groups entitled to claim political asylum while at the same time selling arms to the Turkish government, the CDU press spokesman started a public row by asserting that Grass did not know what he was talking about.[4] The occasion was the award of the Peace Prize of the German Book Trade to Yaşar Kemal and the location once again the highly symbolic Paulskirche in Frankfurt. Grass was taking the fight to a tiring CDU administration on a topic he knew would resonate with sectors of the electorate. His statement was a contribution to the debate about the nation which revolved increasingly around the economy, and thus Grass was laying claim to territory which since the mid-1960s had belonged to writers schooled in the Gruppe 47. It was a basic principle for Grass that Germany, on account of its recent past as a militarized state which brought war to the rest of the world, should not participate in the international arms trade. Because the same Nazi regime persecuted minorities and political opponents who fled abroad, Germany should honour the original article in the Grundgesetz and grant asylum to victims of political oppression. As Kohl was voted out within a year, Grass won this particular skirmish.

Grass remained deeply critical of free-market capitalism as ideology and practice, setting out his views in two key speeches

Grass with Chancellor Gerhard Schröder and sculptor Carl Fredrik Reuterswärd in 2005.

on 'Germany as Economic Location' (1997), in a televised conversation with the French sociologist Pierre Bourdieu in 1999, and 'Freedom According to the Stock Market' (2005).[5] With Daniela Dahn, an *ossi* who championed the 'losers of unification' in a series of hard-hitting reports, and his old associate Johano Strasser, Grass then edited a 600-page book on the effects of inequality on the nation's well-being. It was dedicated to the memory of Pierre Bourdieu, who died in January 2002 and whose comment about the 'terror of the economic' and fear that 'we are witnessing the destruction of European civilization in the name of profit maximization' are quoted in the introduction.[6] When Schröder felt obliged in 2003 to liberalize employment regulations and cut payments to the unemployed in order to bring down the unemployment figures (the so-called 'Agenda 2010'), he faced a revolt from within his own party, from which the SPD has arguably yet to recover. Grass stayed quiet. Schröder's decision earlier in the year not to join the Anglo-American invasion of Iraq made it for Grass a price worth paying.

As a party-political polemicist, Grass was not embroiled in public arguments during the seven years of the red–green coalition from 1998 to 2005. He became as close to Schröder as he had been to any SPD politician of the Brandt–Schmidt era, including Brandt himself.[7] Frenz and Matthiesen's 2007 documentary shows Grass pay a visit to the Kanzleramt in Berlin to fetch Schröder for the opening of an anti-war memorial. For the first time, on Grass's eightieth birthday in 2007, the SPD showed its formal appreciation with a handsomely produced book, officially edited and with a foreword by the party chairman.[8]

With his two main literary publications from this period, Grass was swimming once again in the mainstream. In July 1999, as the capital of Germany was moving from Bonn to Berlin, came *My Century*, a collection of 100 stories, one for each year of the twentieth century. This quite unusual book, which was published simultaneously in an enlarged collector's edition with lavish watercolour illustrations, was received more positively than anything he had published since *The Meeting in Telgte*. It is both an autobiography and a portrait of Germany through the last 100 years, entwining episodes from his own life with that of his epoch and country. Grass is saying, in other words, that the nation can see its true self reflected through the writer and public figure Günter Grass, through my experiences, the lessons which I have drawn, and the related themes and events which I have selected for attention. It is surely unprecedented for a writer to assert ownership over an entire century in this way, though he is said to have been surprised that he alone had this idea in the late 1990s.

My Century was followed three months later by the long-awaited award of the Nobel Prize in Literature, which was a cause for national celebration. 'Nobel Laureate', or *Nobelpreisträger*, became his new epithet and official job description from now on. In February 2002 he published *Crabwalk*, about the tragic evacuation of civilians from Danzig in the winter of 1945. This runaway international best-seller exerted as big an impact on the public imagination in Germany as any book since *The Tin Drum*. If in most respects the elaborately constructed novella is hardly an exciting work of fiction despite some memorable passages, the subject-matter was all the more explosive. Grass now placed the full weight of his accumulated symbolic capital, as Germany's foremost author whose critique of behaviour during and after the Third Reich had for decades been unsparing, behind the public commemoration of the wartime suffering of citizens of the perpetrator nation. This represented a momentous turnaround in his thinking. As recently as *The Call of the Toad* he associated expellees with essentially revanchist aspirations. Fifty-seven years since the defeat of Nazism, there were still millions who could remember 1945 and millions more who had grown up listening to their memories. Grass shifted perceptions of the expellees. At last their plight and experiences in both post-war German states could be acknowledged without prejudice by popular authors such as Andreas Kossert, who quotes Grass liberally in another landmark publication which was widely read at the end of the decade.[9]

My Century contains some of Grass's most lyrical prose. It is a new departure artistically, consisting of a series of short narratives – authorial memoirs, fictional letters and witness statements, and dialogues – each of which both stands by itself while also relating to the rest of the collection, usually through its theme. Fifteen chapters are directly autobiographical and narrated in the first person. Five of these are stand-alones: '1927', which is more about his mother's brief enjoyment of the 'golden twenties' than his own birth; '1937', in which he recalls how he and his schoolmates played at being General Franco in the Spanish Civil War; '1953', when he and Anna witnessed the 17 June Uprising in East Berlin; '1959', which consists of a single two-page sentence in which they danced through the news that *The Tin Drum* was taking the world by storm; and '1965', about his first election tour for Brandt. The other ten are in three clusters: 1975 to 1977 cover the writers' meetings in East Berlin; 1988 to 1990 take in his and Ute's visit to Calcutta, followed by *waldsterben*, or dying forest syndrome brought on by acid rain, and reunification; and 1996 to 1998 culminate in the red–green election victory, while '1999' is narrated by his resurrected mother, who effectively presides over the entire century, at last able to enjoy her son's success. The majority of the autobiographical chapters are thus about Grass the writer in the public domain.

There are three other clusters, covering the two world wars, 1914 to 1918 and 1939 to 1945, and the period of student protest, 1966 to 1968. All but three of the non-autobiographical chapters are narrated by a usually unidentified fictional witness to a great event or participant in a trend-setting phenomenon. '1906' is by Arthur Conan Doyle's fictional u-boat commander Captain Sirius.[10] Three well-known non-fictional narrators are, in '1911', Kaiser Wilhelm; in '1974', Günter Guillaume, whose exposure as a spy at the heart of Brandt's government resulted in his resignation; and in '1994', Birgit Breuel, the successor to Rohwedder as the head of the Treuhand and to whom Grass now gives an opportunity to respond to her critical portrayal in *Too Far Afield*.

The trick in many chapters is to invent an oblique or unexpected perspective on an aspect of German history which itself is more or less well known. The narrative viewpoint sometimes stands in contradistinction to the subject-matter and can rarely be conflated with Grass's own. This often results in a version of 'history from below', which was an integral part of Grass's project from *The Tin Drum* through *The Flounder* to *Too Far Afield*. As a literary method it is hardly original but he aims to unsettle his readers with challenging combinations. The chapter '1993', for example, is the tale of a low-ranking policeman from the old East reflecting on the wave of racist attacks which began when a Rostock centre for asylum seekers was besieged and set on fire in August 1991. The policeman concludes that such behaviour approximates to the norm in Western Europe and the usA and there is no point in making a big fuss about it. The '1970' chapter details Brandt's historic mission to Warsaw when he fell spontaneously to his knees in front of the monument to the Jewish victims of the Warsaw Ghetto and is narrated by a journalist who is hostile to the SPD chancellor.

If *My Century* is to work, the effect on the reader has to be cumulative; the book has to add up to more than the sum of its parts. One way of assessing it would be through a statistical analysis of narrators and themes. Which stories are recorded, how many are devoted to German culpability, for example, and how many to the Holocaust, and whom Grass chooses to set down their versions are all vitally important questions. At last there are fictional women narrators.

My Century was published in the wake of the controversy surrounding Daniel Goldhagen's *Hitler's Willing Executioners*.[11] It is to some degree a native response to an American account of German history in the same way that in the 1980s Edgar Reitz's television series *Heimat* was a response to the Hollywood melodrama *Holocaust*. Memory debates raged in unified Germany at the beginning of the new century and they took many forms. Anne Fuchs and Mary Cosgrove enumerate the following topics: the meaning of Auschwitz (in the so-called Walser-Bubis debate), the touring Wehrmacht exhibition, the protracted decision over the Holocaust memorial in Berlin, the relevance of 1968 and the legacy of the Stasi.[12] If the emphasis with respect to the Nazi past had been placed on confrontation following a period of denial and repression, it was now on reconciliation between the generations and commemoration.[13]

The '1901' chapter is narrated from the late 1950s by an anonymous collector who has stumbled across an undelivered postcard written from Palestine by the poet Else Lasker-Schüler to Gottfried Benn in 1945, in which she recalls the opening of the famous hover-rail in her native Wuppertal at the beginning of the century. Real history is somehow suspended in this story as a bridge is built between a Jewish exile (Lasker-Schüler) and her

Expressionist colleague (Benn), a former lover who stayed in Germany, initially attempting to work with the Nazis. Grass treats the Holocaust explicitly in '1938', in which a school history teacher looks back from 1990 to remind his class that 9 November 1989 was the 51st anniversary of the November Pogrom or Kristallnacht – he could have added that it was the date the Weimar Republic was founded in 1918, which is why Hitler chose it for his so-called Beer Hall Putsch in 1923. Chapter '1962' is told by a Jewish native of Nuremberg who built the bulletproof glass cage in which Adolf Eichmann sat during his trial in Jerusalem after being kidnapped by the Israeli secret service. He fled from Germany with his little brother to Palestine in 1938 and they are the only two family members to survive. Chapter '1964' is told by a Frankfurt woman who by chance came to sit in the audience at the Auschwitz Trials which took place that year. There are some other Jewish themes and figures. Adorno and Celan have chapters to themselves and the book is dedicated to the memory of Jakob Suhl, who appears in '1990' when he returns for the first time to his native Leipzig on the day of the first free elections in the still-existing GDR.

Grass was expanding the literary tradition of the 'calendar' or 'almanac story', as practised by Grimmelshausen, Johann Peter Hebel in the early 1800s and Bertolt Brecht.[14] By imagining witnesses to historical phenomena who often recall their role decades after the action is over, he shows that the meaning of a particular historical event often only becomes clear many years after it has happened. Unlike Hebel and Brecht's witnesses, Grass's tend to have an understanding of the wider history they are living through. Time is as always the constitutive element through which meaning is generated and human beings can understand their experiences. What happened can be less important than how we remember what happened. Hebel's most famous story, 'Unexpected Reunion', is about a miner who is killed at work the day before his wedding around the year 1750. The reader then hears how his fiancée lives her long life in parallel to a series of wars, political events and natural disasters. Before she dies a spinster in old age, the miner's perfectly preserved young corpse comes to light and she sees him one last time. It is a much anthologized story and was discussed or adapted by numerous twentieth-century German writers, including Walter Benjamin, Ernst Bloch, Elias Canetti, Uwe Johnson and W. G. Sebald (and more recently was the inspiration for David Constantine's short story, which was adapted for the screen as *45 Years* by Andrew Haigh in 2015, starring Tom Courtenay and Charlotte Rampling). Grass cites Hebel's name only once in a list of German authors in *Headbirths* (VII:124) but he echoed 'Unexpected Reunion' in *The Flounder* when Sophie Rotzoll was reunited with Friedrich Bartholdy after he spent 38 years in a Danzig prison for revolutionary agitation aged seventeen.

The whole century is by necessity viewed from its conclusion and the authorial persona inhabits all the different voices, as he writes in the first line: 'I changing places with myself was present year after year.' There are numerous cross-references across the decades, which show how the past can come back to life at unexpected moments (much like Hebel's embalmed miner). Thus the Second World War is narrated by a reporter who recalls at a meeting in 1962 how he filed propagandist copy from numerous fronts during the conflict.

Grass is particularly interested in divided loyalties and split identities. So '1922' is narrated by an informer from inside the Organisation Consul which assassinated foreign minister Walter Rathenau. He disagrees with assassination as a policy and each time tries to warn the state and the politicians themselves, but nobody listens to him. And '1934' is a similar account of the murder of the anarchist writer Erich Mühsam in Oranienburg concentration camp by the SA adjutant who delegated the task of killing him to a subordinate who failed to do a clean job. The narrator is irritated by the situation but most of all disconcerted by Mühsam's bravery under interrogation and habit of smiling at his tormentors while quoting classical verse back at them. Chapter '1972' is by the left-wing teacher who reported that two suspicious persons, one of whom turned out to be the wanted terrorist Ulrike Meinhof, were lodging in his flat. In '1974' Günter Guillaume is uncertain which German team to cheer when the GDR play the FRG in the World Cup, which took place that year in West Germany. The hosts eventually won the competition but lost this particular first-round match. Sport is never just about sport. Sporting contests accrue meanings through the complex set of circumstances in which they are played and followed. Yet the focus on topics such as sport indicate a growing sense of a normalized view of history.

Reviewers on the whole recognized that *My Century* was an intrinsically German book, but they did not like its didactic impulse, some seeing it as a Sunday-school lesson in social democracy.[15] There are three strategically placed chapters on the SPD to add to Grass's memoir of the 1965 campaign: '1928' is from the perspective of a mother of three grown-up sons, two of whom are killed in political street fighting, on the party's defeat by an unholy alliance of the extreme right and the extreme left; '1970' about Brandt in Warsaw; and the penultimate chapter, '1998', gives Grass's version of the red–green victory. This second electoral switch from centre-right to centre-left under Grass's beloved vehicle for progressive politics, the Social Democratic Party, which immediately precedes the final chapter narrated by his proud mother, enables him to end on a conciliatory note.

Three months after *My Century* was published came news of the Nobel award. At home and abroad, Grass was a popular choice. He scrubbed up in a brand-new morning suit for the ceremony in Oslo, gave an insightful speech about literary history and the purpose of imaginative narrative, and was snapped partnering his daughter Helene on the dance floor. It was the first time that a German citizen had won the prize since Heinrich Böll in 1972 (Elias

Canetti, who won in 1981, wrote in German but by the time he was honoured by the Nobel committee he was a British citizen). When informed of his success 27 years ago, Böll is reputed to have asked: 'why not Grass?' Even Marcel Reich-Ranicki agreed that the award to Grass was overdue. In 1972 the Federal Republic was polarized by the threat posed by the Red Army Faction and by its supposed sympathizers in the intelligentsia. Sections of the popular press saw the Nobel award to Böll as an example of a foreign body supporting an unwelcome critic of the state. It was a sign of how far Germany had matured as a democracy that this allegation was not repeated with respect to Grass in 1999, especially as his critique of unification was more fundamental than Böll's call for calm and understanding in the early 1970s.

Then, in early 2002, as he prepared to mark his 75th birthday, came *Crabwalk*. A short novel by Anglo-Saxon standards, a 'novella' in German terms, he had originally considered the same title for *The Call of the Toad*. It denotes his understanding that history moves forward in a roundabout movement which includes retreats and detours. Calling it a novella achieves two things. It makes a link with *Cat and Mouse*, which is his only other such work of short fiction – *The Meeting in Telgte* and *The Call of the Toad*, while comparable in scope, are *erzählungen* (tales or narratives). And it draws attention to the narrative framing, which is an essential component of novella narration, from Boccaccio to the German classics of the nineteenth century. *Cat and Mouse* also features the adolescent Tulla Pokriefke, who takes centre stage in *Crabwalk* – now in her mid-seventies. As in *Cat and Mouse*, it is the teller and his telling of his tale which is at the centre of Grass's attention. That tale concerns the largest maritime disaster in history, the sinking of the former *Strength-through-Joy* cruise liner the *Wilhelm Gustloff* by a Soviet submarine on the night of 30 January 1945 – the liner was holding up to 10,000 passengers, mostly civilian refugees, the great majority of whom perished. It is quickly told. The catastrophe was one of several sinkings in the

Baltic Sea, as millions of people from West and East Prussia, Danzig and Pomerania left their homes to flee the advancing Red Army, many of them choosing the apparently quicker option of evacuation by water in preference to an overland trek.

The *Gustloff* held a special place in Grass's own memory, as it did in the collective memory of the expellees. At the end of the war when he wondered whether he was going to see his family again, one possibility was that they had been on board. There are ample signs that the disaster remained on the edges of his imaginative vision throughout his writing career. In *Crabwalk* he corrects that. He first mentioned the *Gustloff* in *The Tin Drum* as the Matzeraths' neighbours Herr and Frau Scheffler took a holiday on the prestigious ship on the eve of the war. In Schlöndorff's film, for which Grass helped with the script, Frau Scheffler is heard to say just before the Red Army soldiers overrun Oskar's family in their shop cellar that she is leaving on the *Gustloff*. In *Dog Years,* most of Matern's family drown in the evacuation, as did Starusch's mother in *Local Anaesthestic*, though the ships they sailed on are not named. In *The Rat*, the *Gustloff* is one of a number of ships which are sunk in the last days of the war in the Baltic; others were transporting concentration camp prisoners, which Grass cites as analogies to spaceship earth, which is heading for a similar disaster. Next to the firestorm which engulfed Danzig's historic old city, the *Gustloff* encapsulates the catastrophe of the Second World War, which was ever present in his creative and moral imagination.

The narrator of *Crabwalk* is Paul Pokriefke, son of Tulla who was born in a rescue boat that very night, making him literally a child of the disaster. His seventeen-year-old mother's hair turned white that instant. Paul rehearses his account of the voyage, the preparations for it and the ship's torpedoing precisely halfway through the novella, which takes up to 20 per cent of the total narrative space. Paul grew up hearing his mother's telling of it, usually on Saturday evenings, and consequently he knows her version off by heart.

He acts now as her editorial filter, telling the tale of her telling the tale but at the same time commenting on his son Konrad's neo-Nazi version, which Konrad is publishing simultaneously on the Internet. Since being commissioned by 'the old man', a fictional cipher for the author Günter Grass, Paul has researched the events of that night, making his knowledge much more rounded than his mother's and his son's. He has read books by Heinz Schön, for example, an eighteen-year-old assistant purser in January 1945 with the good fortune to survive who devoted the rest of his life to telling the world what happened, assisting too on the first film, entitled *Night Fell over Gotenhafen*, which was released in 1959. The *Gustloff* was never by any means repressed history, but it did not fit into a progressive narrative in either German state. In the GDR nobody wanted to be reminded that German civilians had been sent to their deaths by a Soviet U-boat. In the FRG the disaster belonged to the expellees who struggled to reconcile themselves with the new German border in the East. Tulla's version, relayed in her original Danzig dialect, retains its authenticity and appears to have been remarkably clear and unusually free from rancour and resentment. In other respects, Tulla is an unstable character, alternating from one extreme set of beliefs to another and never able to settle down with a partner.

Paul deals economically with controversies in the historiography, which have always centred on blame and responsibility. There were as many as four captains on the bridge, for example, who were not agreed on the best route or whether to keep the ship's lights on. Most of the rescue boats could not be launched as a consequence of inadequate preparation. Painted grey and carrying military personnel, the *Gustloff* was a legitimate military target. The evacuation was chaotically carried out and with a high degree of incompetence, but in addition to its military cargo, the ship carried more than 4,000 children and thousands of adult civilians. Grass allows himself the poetic licence of a metaphor only when it comes to the vessel's final moments, and Tulla is convinced that she heard a long, dull but penetrating scream echo across the icy swell.

The remainder of *Crabwalk*, up to four-fifths of the total text, embeds the disaster in a series of interlocking contexts, both at the beginning of the new century, when Paul finally commits his account to paper, and in the history of the Third Reich. Paul is fascinated that 30 January should be the date of the sinking in 1945, the date in 1933 on which Hitler was appointed Reichskanzler by Hindenburg and the birthday in 1895 of the Nazi martyr Wilhelm Gustloff after whom the ship was named. Paul traces Gustloff's career before he was murdered by the Jewish anti-Nazi resistor David Frankfurter in Chur in Switzerland in 1936. He explains the Nazi Strength-through-Joy programme – which was intended to ensure that workers enjoyed access to holidays and leisure-time activities – and recounts how the *Gustloff*'s pre-war cruises benefitted members of the working population. He finds out about Frankfurter's motivation and sketches the war and post-war career of the Russian submarine captain Marinesko, who gave the order to fire the three torpedoes. This history is well known or at least straightforward to research. Gustloff's murder was written up straight away by the popular exiled writer Emil Ludwig. Grass then adds a contemporary layer of complication because Konrad becomes interested in reclaiming the history of both Gustloff the man and the ship named after him.

Konrad was named after Tulla's younger brother, who could neither speak nor hear and whose drowning resulted in her seven 'dog days' of mourning. This makes Konrad a second-generation victim of his grandmother's trauma. Tulla then radicalizes him when he reaches the fateful age of seventeen and becomes embroiled in an online argument with a youth calling himself 'David', after Gustloff's murderer. 'David' turns out to be a contemporary whose real name is Wolfgang Stremplin, who over-identifies with the Nazis' Jewish victims to the extent of renaming himself and assuming a Jewish identity. In the end he offers himself up to be killed by Konrad in a bizarre act of atonement for Nazi crimes on 20 April 1997. Konrad is jailed for manslaughter but by the time his father writes his book there are signs that he has learnt a lesson. He was seventeen at the time of the murder, the age in Grass's fiction for hot-headed actions and unquestioning belief in a cause.

It was less these contexts than the enclosed narrative of the sinking which initiated national discussions lasting for months and generated a remarkable academic industry, as *Crabwalk* dominated the best-seller lists.[16] It inspired another film, a television two-parter which was part of a series of popular made-for-TV dramatizations of German Second World War history. Germany had at last found a way to accommodate the suffering of its own people into a narrative which was neither revanchist nor chauvinist. When asked her opinion on publication of the English version, Eva Figes said:

> Times have changed, and as a German Jew I feel it's time to put the other side and take a more sophisticated view of the war rather than divide everybody into goodies and baddies. Clearly ordinary Germans suffered catastrophe towards the end. I used to get uptight when Germans said, 'We also suffered'. I don't feel that any more.[17]

Once again, Grass led a shift in attitudes towards the history of the recently concluded century and his reach was international. This made the disappointment at the revelation of his SS membership in his next major work all the more acute.

8

The Culmination of Project Self

Grass's last big project consists of three very different books, making what has been termed a 'valedictory', 'memory' or 'autobiographical' trilogy.[1] *Peeling the Onion* (2006) covers the twenty years between the outbreak of war in 1939 and the publication of *The Tin Drum*. In *The Box* (2008) he imagines his eight children and stepchildren discussing their memories of him between the mid-1960s and the mid-1990s, with the help of photographs taken with the old-fashioned box camera of the title. *Grimms' Words* (2010) intersperses memories of his political campaigning with an account of the brothers Grimm setting about compiling their famous dictionary after their expulsion from Göttingen University for protesting against the King of Saxony's curtailing of the constitution. If his novels are interwoven with autobiography, these three memoirs are mixed with fiction, though each volume adopts a radically different approach to its subject, as I will try to show. The trilogy took Grass between seven and eight years to complete, the same time as his first three prose works and the middle sequence which began with *From the Diary of a Snail* and concluded with *Headbirths*. It marks yet again, but for the last time, both a new departure and a return to his beginnings.

There were practical reasons for choosing autobiography. Turning 75 in 2002, Grass was aware of the need to conserve energy. One advantage of literary self-reflection is that no research is necessary. For *Grimms' Words* he drew on his reading of a handful of primary and secondary sources by or about the brothers Grimm and their circle, which included in particular Bettina von Arnim, who becomes the first historical female writer whose work ever caught his attention. She has a walk-on part in *The Flounder*, but only in relation to three creative men, as the sister of one poet, the future wife of another and the biographer of a third. Now, she drives the action forward and is presented as an author to be taken seriously.

Grass was also writing poetry throughout this late period. His last two decades are by some margin his most prolific as a poet, with no fewer than six volumes produced between 1993 and 2015. Like his prose after *Too Far Afield*, they are all accompanied by extensive artwork on matching themes and published first as hardbacks with Steidl's trademark high production values. While he had always written poems, in contrast to drama which he gave up in 1969, they became enmeshed with his prose projects, such as *The Flounder*, *The Rat*, *Show Your Tongue* and the *Studio Reports*.[2] *Novemberland* (1993) was astoundingly his first book of poems since *Questioned Out* (1967) and was followed by *Lost and Found Items for Non-readers* (1997), *Last Dances* (2003), *Silly Clown* (2007), *Mayflies* (2012) and the posthumous *Of All That Ends* (2015), in which he mingles verse with both drawings and short prose. Memory and mortality are prominent themes but what is more striking is that he eschews the obscure, highly personal imagery which characterized much of the poetry published in the 1950s and 1960s. His late poetic style is personal and confessional, in contrast. Could it be that he unpacked the imagery in his earlier poetry in a great cycle of prose works which began with *The Tin Drum* and concluded more or less with *The Rat*? It was certainly remarkable that just about each of them could be traced back to images or motifs he first sketched out in his twenties or early thirties. From *Too Far Afield* onwards this is no longer the case.

Writing autobiography, however, represented something of a turnaround, even a climb-down in Grass's thinking. He had always dismissed the genre, arguing either that it entailed an

Grass with publisher Gerhard Steidl and secretary Hilke Ohsoling examining artwork for *Peeling the Onion*, Behlendorf, 2006.

outmoded belief in a unified personality or that all that focus on the self diverted attention from the world outside.[3] Unlike authors of autobiography, he wanted to get out into that world and have an impact on it with his writing. This was a bizarre line to take given that he constantly transformed memories and experiences into fiction; considering his secret past as a Waffen-ss recruit, the declarations now risk sounding insincere. It is also simply not true that he eschewed the genre entirely. He often summarized his life or recalled episodes from it in speeches and public statements, from the poem 'Kleckerburg' (1965) and 'Speech to a Young Voter Who Feels Tempted to Vote for the NPD' (1966) to the public exchange of letters with the Japanese writer, Kenzaburo Oe (1995). He wrote mini-memoirs in the form of essays or lectures ('Looking back on *The Tin Drum*', 1973; 'Writing after Auschwitz', 1990; 'The Learning Teacher', 1999), travelogues (*Headbirths* and *Show Your Tongue*) and published diaries of two politically pivotal years (*From the Diary of a Snail* and *From Germany to Germany: Diary of 1990*). He was in fact a prolific diarist – the date these diaries will be published or made available to researchers is not likely to come for some years, however.

As readers discovered when his correspondence with Helen Wolff was published in 2003, Grass wrote annual résumés of his activities to his German-speaking American confidante. Much of the material in *Peeling the Onion*, as well as the private episodes in *The Box* and the more public reminiscences in *Grimms' Words*, were already familiar to his more dedicated readers. There are always variations in the repetitions, however.

There were also interviews and his collaboration with his biographers. Grass's first book-length interview from 1979 – with the French writer Nicole Casanova – begins with a declaration that would not look out of place in *Peeling the Onion*, to the effect that he cannot be entirely trusted when he recounts episodes from his past because each time he will tell a different version. The trope is familiar from his fiction: Oskar admits on the first page of *The Tin Drum* that he 'tells lies' in the name of art. Grass had told stories since childhood and anyone who took him at his word was a fool. According to his account of his literary beginnings, his entire career was anticipated in childhood. His mother was his first and ideal listener. As he recalls in *Peeling the Onion*, she called him Peer Gynt because he was always making things up. There are some signs that *Atelier des métamorphoses* (Studio of Transformations), as Casanova entitled their encounter, which stretched over several months in the autumn of 1977, was ahead of its time. German readers were not yet ready for an autobiography by Grass. A summary of Casanova's book was translated in *Der Spiegel*, but presented as a single continuous interview which repeated already familiar tropes rather than divulging new material, such as his mother's experience of rape at the end of the war. [4]

Grass dates his interest in writing about his youth to a lecture he gave about 'the future of memory' in 2000 in the Lithuanian capital Vilnius. He was invited, along with three other writers including Czesław Miłosz, by the head of the Lithuanian Goethe-Institut to discuss the meaning of memory in a part of Europe which had experienced violent upheaval and genocide in the twentieth century. Grass made a memorable formulation about brushing 'the cat of memory' in the wrong direction until it began to purr.[5] This better describes the technique in his next book *Crabwalk* than *Peeling the Onion*, however.

Grass's reflections on his own past intensify in the late 1990s. As well as *My Century*, 1999 saw the publication of *The Adventures of the Enlightenment*, another book-length interview-cum-collaborative-memoir, arranged in a chronological sequence by the author and radio journalist Harro Zimmermann. In 2001 biographer Michael Jürgs gained extensive interview access, on which he based much of his account of Grass's war years. None of the material was new, which Jürgs appears not to have noticed, and much of it would resurface in *Peeling the Onion*, except that Grass did not give Jürgs the detail of his SS membership, reserving that for his own publication.

Volker Neuhaus detects an unwillingness to settle down and write *Peeling the Onion* even once he had decided to do so.[6] If the hostility of the press reaction surprised him and he was wounded by what he saw as the perfidy of the *Frankfurter Allgemeine Zeitung*, or FAZ, in leading on the SS revelation after a pre-publication interview, Grass knew that he was going to face criticism for his 'confession'. A draft first line of *Crabwalk* explains that he hesitated to broach the potentially controversial subject of that book in case doing so would have necessitated 'owning up to everything'. Once the reaction to *Peeling the Onion* had been framed by the FAZ, Grass was subjected to an onslaught of criticism in both Germany and abroad. This was new since Grass scandals had up to now been home-grown affairs. The FAZ journalist Frank Schirrmacher was an astute commentator on literary affairs and a consummate operator in the world of cultural politics. He made his name in 1990 by first dismissing post-war West German writing as politically motivated (*gesinnungsliteratur*) and took a lead in attacking Christa Wolf in 1992 when her brief collaboration with the Stasi came to light. His skewering of Grass was a masterclass and the latest episode in a post-unification culture war which began in the heady days of 1990.[7]

August 2006 showed once again that Grass could command attention across the globe. He would do so on one further occasion before his death, with the poem 'What Has to Be Said' about German arms shipments to Israel, which was published in April 2012 and led to accusations of anti-Semitism, which seemed all the easier to make after *Peeling the Onion*. Ever the showman with a new book to sell, it seemed to some that the revelation was calculated, but Grass immediately lost all control of the book's reception, as he had in the case of *Too Far Afield*, and the personal criticisms clearly stung him, as they always did.

The disclosure seemed to fit a familiar schema: 'Leading Figure Is Revealed to Have Nazi Connections'. Kurt Waldheim, the former secretary-general to the United Nations, set the pattern when it was revealed in 1986 on his standing to be president of Austria that as a young Wehrmacht officer he had known more about the Holocaust than he was ready to admit. There are two differences: Grass never lied, he just avoided spelling out one small part of the truth; and he also revealed the key information himself rather than being confronted with it. It was also a secret which he had shared from time to time with writer colleagues. While Eva Menasse was annoyed that he had not confided in the writers who first met in Lübeck in 2005 when Grass read from the manuscript of *Peeling the Onion*, Robert Schindel, the leading Jewish writer in Austria, was *au courant*, for instance.[8]

Grass now did what he had done in the autumn of 1995 after the reception of *Too Far Afield*: he retreated from the public eye and said nothing, giving an account of his actions only to the city president of Gdańsk, Paweł Adamowicz, in a public letter in which he explained:

in the decades after the war, as I came to know of the terrible extent of Waffen-SS war crimes, I did not repress this brief but incriminating episode in my youth but out of shame I kept it to myself. Only now in my old age have I found the words to report on it in a larger context. My silence can be judged a mistake and – as is happening now – be condemned.[9]

Calls for him to be stripped of his honorary citizenship of Gdańsk soon subsided. When *Peeling the Onion* appeared in Polish, the city was excited – taxi drivers were eager to identify the many Danzig locations which he describes. Adamowicz was quoted in late August in the German press: 'Danzig understands its son.'[10]

Should the belated confession of his SS past make us reassess his literary writing and/or his public standing? These are two different questions which require different answers. His secret must have helped him as a writer, and not just with some of his plots. Novelists tend not to be individuals who are entirely at ease with themselves or with the world at large, which is why they write in the first place. Several of Grass's main characters feel a sense of guilt for past actions which is out of proportion to what they actually did. They also often have secrets, as well as give multiple versions of past events, evolving evasive coping strategies when it comes to their wartime past. What overwhelmed Grass was the understanding of what he *could* so easily have done, if he had been just a little older. If he had joined the same SS division in 1942, say, he would not have lacked opportunities to involve himself in mass shootings and other atrocities. It disturbed him that he did not ask questions, about his uncle Frantizek who was shot or about a classmate who disappeared, one of whom he now discusses in *Peeling the Onion*. He was also perplexed by the Jehovah's Witness during his Labour Service who refused to hold a rifle and was disturbed that he joined in the bullying of him with the other boys who shared their barracks. There are also secrets and biographical mysteries in his fiction. What is it precisely that is gnawing away at the nameless narrator of *The Call of the Toad*? Why are both 'the old man' and Paul Pokriefke so hard on themselves in *Crabwalk*?

His public reputation is a somewhat different matter. His image and brand name were damaged perhaps irreparably, which he was the last to recognize, blaming a bout of collective self-righteousness in the media. His self-pity in a suite of poems in *Silly Clown*, which came out the following year, did little to rescue the situation.[11] The suspicion that he would not have won the Nobel Prize had the truth been out earlier was all the more irksome for being impossible to counter. Six years later he was the last person in Germany who could get away with a provocative statement about Israel, whether in verse or any other medium. Grass sent the poem 'What Has to Be Said' (without showing it to his editor) to the *Süddeutsche Zeitung* (after *Die Zeit* turned it down) and syndicated it across continental Europe to *La Repubblica*, *El País* and *Le Monde*. What could his readers think except that he had either lost the plot or

Poster seen in Göttingen two months after Grass's death in June 2015: 'Shut up!' 'With my last ink? Just enough left for anti-Semitism!'

forgotten how the media worked? The explanation is a little more complicated. Grass's interventions were always gambits in an elaborate game of self-presentation as the country's most famous author taking a public stand, as Stuart Taberner helpfully elucidated with respect to 'What Has to Be Said'.[12] The gambit backfired this time because Grass had not grasped that the perception of his image had changed since 2006. Once again, it came down to the framing. A poem in *Last Dances* about the role of African Americans in the U.S. armed forces, 'Military Blues' (1:365–6), has greater potential to offend but nobody appears to have noticed it.

Like *Too Far Afield*, the first instalment in the autobiographical trilogy stands in the shadow of its critical reception, which relates only to a single detail in it. It is a piece of life writing of remarkable quality and was well received as such, the 'scandal' of the SS confession notwithstanding, providing his publishers with another best-seller, soon translated into more than a dozen languages. Like *The Rat* and *My Century*, *Peeling the Onion* has no generic designation, leaving readers to wonder: is it fact or fiction, a memoir or an auto-biographical novel, or is it impossible to make such distinctions? There are multiple cross-overs with the fiction, in particular with *The Tin Drum*, *Cat and Mouse*, *Dog Years*, *Local Anaesthetic*, *My Century* and *Crabwalk*, and when it comes to the topography of Danzig with *The Flounder* and *The Rat*. *Peeling the Onion* is the most traditional of the autobiographical trilogy, covering family, school and extracurricula education, first love and subsequent romantic escapades. Thomas Bernhard and Elias Canetti, Arthur Schnitzler and Theodor Fontane, all wrote similar accounts of their most formative years. The original model in German is Goethe's *Dichtung und Wahrheit*, which accounts for his first quarter of a century until he wrote *The Sorrows of Young Werther* and became famous.

Grass has lots of good material and is back on his favoured terrain. The episodes are pieced together into a chronological sequence but they often remain fragments. There are many which his readers will recognize: the reading material he consumed from his mother's bookcase, the parable of his three uncles, his expulsions from two schools, the Conradinum and the Petri-Oberschule, his bewilderment at the behaviour of the pacifist Jehovah's Witness, observation of the Jewish Ben and the German Dieter, two seventeen-year-olds in a camp for displaced persons whose plight Grass dares to compare, the attack on his company by 'Stalin Wurlitzers' in April 1945, the post-war visit to Dachau and his overhearing political discussions down the potash mine. The memorable story about the hotel chef from Bessarabia in the Bad Aibling POW camp, who gives beginners' cookery lessons to an assembled class of fellow prisoners using entirely imaginary ingredients and utensils, is first told with minor variations in *Local Anaesthetic*.

He includes other stories which are almost certainly made up. The tale of how he carried a pot of coffee every morning to his NCO, carefully pausing each time behind a tree to urinate into it, sounds like fiction, like a deed which he would like to claim as his own but which he almost certainly did not commit. Once again, he is experimenting with an alternative self. Whether or not it happened is impossible to verify one way or the other. The past has as many skins as an onion, which are peeled back one after the other to reveal a non-existent centre. The story about meeting a contemporary called Joseph in the POW camp comes into the category of fiction. The seventeen-year-old is the future Bavarian cleric Joseph Ratzinger (born April 1927), who was made pope in 2005. Ratzinger is an alter ego of sorts, his path through life running in parallel to Grass's own, except that he chose religion rather than literature and stuck to a faith which Grass rejected.

Other material is also new to his readers, though probably not to family or friends. They knew his explanation for not wanting to learn to ride a bicycle: not being able to do so saved his life during hand-to-hand fighting with Soviet troops. He finds himself in a recently abandoned cycle shop with half a dozen other frightened recruits and a sergeant. At the sergeant's orders the recruits all grab a bicycle to make a dash for it, leaving the only non-cyclist to cover them with his machine gun. He rues his inability to ride a bike, convinced that his parents' poverty will now cost him his life, but the opposite turns out to be the case as the cyclists are mown down in the middle of the road, leaving him the sole lucky survivor. Grass may have not told any portion of this story in print before, but Hermann Ott in *From the Diary of a Snail* takes refuge in a cycle shop owned by Anton Stomma. It is a powerful, poignant tale which gives added force to his conviction that his survival was purely down to chance and one of the reasons that he both writes and tries to affect the world through other means is that the dead are looking over his shoulder. His lifelong admiration for Grimmelshausen's *Simplicissimus*, whose hero believes himself to be at the mercy of Lady Fortune as he negotiates his way through the Thirty Years' War, takes on a new dimension. Grass's sensibility is 'baroque' in that he can see death in life; his enjoyment of food and sex is heightened by his awareness that he is alive through luck.

Some critics have found *Peeling the Onion* to be two books in one, bracketing off the post-war episodes when he becomes the hero of his own picaresque novel.[13] This is only true if 'memory politics' is the primary focus. There is, for sure, plenty which he misses out or skates over, his intellectual influences as he prepared to write his first novel being a frustrating gap, as Neuhaus complains.[14] The three hungers which he experiences acutely in the POW camp and which determine his biographical trajectory and his literary work go some way to explaining his whole life and oeuvre. He yearns for food, which explains his passion for cooking and conviviality, both in life and in fiction – all those imaginary meals with historical figures which can distil the drama of an encounter or advance the action by bringing the truth to the surface. He is hungry for sex (in German *liebe*, which is also the word for love), another sensual pleasure, this time experienced through his penis, which is forever seeking 'redemption'. And he wants art, both to make it and to see or read it, but above all he is desperate to become an artist, to practise art – first sculpture, then drawing and watercolours, poetry and finally prose. Like food and sex, art is a source of pleasure.

The Box followed exactly two years later in 2008 and its reception was altogether quieter. It is probably a lesser book and remarkable less for the contents than the methodology. Instead of continuing to explore his memory of his past selves, as readers could have expected in a sequel to *Peeling the Onion*, Grass imagines summoning his grown-up children and stepchildren to take turns in hosting gatherings to discuss their memories of their famous father or stepfather. He had told Figes in June 1974: 'One day when I am old and beyond good and evil I will write a book which will make you laugh and cry on the subject of my extended family.'[15] At this point he had five children from two mothers. By 2008 there are children aged between thirty and fifty, most of whom are already parents: three boys and a girl from his marriage with Anna Schwarz, two daughters from liaisons with Veronika Schröter and Ingrid Krüger and two stepsons from his marriage with Ute Grunert. A little like Fonty with Madeleine, he felt obliged to keep the youngest daughter's existence a secret for several years, at least from his other children. By imagining how they may see him he tries to see a fictionalized version of himself from the outside. What makes *The Box* interesting as an exercise in autobiography is the way that Grass places himself in the narrative as both authorial figure and subject. He is both in control, insofar as the whole enterprise is his idea, and at the children's discursive mercy as the father is not present at their eight meetings, which are recorded and transcribed and narrated in the third person.

The Grass children are helped by a family friend called Marie, based on the photographer Maria Rama (1911–1997), who uses an ancient Box Brownie camera to take photographs of Grass and his family and close friends over a period of some three decades. Grass worked with Maria Rama on the book *Inmarypraise* (1973), but their association was more productive than that volume of photographs and narrative poem indicate. The Akademie der Künste in Berlin holds some 2,000 photographs in the Maria Rama Collection, the great majority of them taken by her. According to the fiction of *The Box*, Marie's camera also helped him with his succession of creative projects from *Dog Years* to *The Rat*, opening a door to memory and imagination and capturing images of concealed realities. Marie thus assisted the children's father with his writing projects. Her photographs can reveal the past, enabling him to visualize the tavern in Telgte which served as the venue for the writers' meeting in 1647 but which is now concreted over and turned into a car park. They show dreams, fears and fantasies.

At first reading, *The Box* may seem whimsically self-indulgent, presenting what looks like private family history for public consumption. Grass says that he wrote it in a 'happy mood' but after showing his children a draft, some were far from happy with the role assigned to them.[16] He reacted to some of their objections by disguising their names, albeit lightly. None of his biological offspring was appearing in their father's oeuvre for the first time, however. He used to give Helen Wolff a fatherly summary of their activities and his concerns and their letters appeared in 2003. *From the Diary of a Snail* includes conversations with Franz, Raoul, Laura and Bruno about the rise of the Nazis in Danzig during his own childhood, which he first recorded in a lecture entitled 'Difficulties of a Father Explaining Auschwitz to His Children' (1970, XI:591–4). In *From the Diary of a Snail* they ask him questions about the Holocaust which he connects with his obligation to support Willy Brandt and endeavours to answer in simple terms, inventing the story of Hermann Ott as an unlikely example of someone who behaved decently. To the extent that it is based on Veronika Schröter's pregnancy and includes a fictional account of Helene's

Maria Rama in the Algarve, 1987.

birth, *The Flounder* makes arguably greater use of family history:
the dedicatee 'Helene Grass' is either his mother or new daughter.
The '1996' chapter in *My Century* is an account of a spring holiday
in Italy with his three daughters from three different mothers:
Laura, Helene and Nele. It anticipates one theme of *The Box* directly
because, as both father and author, he is concerned here that he

is becoming displaced. The chapter begins with the admission that he intended to write about the cloned sheep twins born that year, whose reproductive history, if transferred to humans, would make fathers redundant. He is nervous about holidaying with his daughters, at first hesitating to lecture them on Italian old masters until he finds he can allegorize them as the three graces. By the end of the chapter his faith in the value of fatherhood is restored by the sight of a large flock of un-cloned sheep in what he takes to be natural formation, led by a ram.

In *The Box*, the father has a nagging fear that his children will recall that he did not pay them enough attention as they were growing up. He was either upstairs at his writing desk or in his studio, absorbed in a conversation with himself about his latest project. Or he was away giving speeches in election campaigns. The younger daughters both grew up with their mothers and when he and Anna separated, the children stayed with her until the youngest complained so forcefully that he came to live with his father and stepmother. The theme of guilt thus links *The Box* with *Peeling the Onion* and although the reason he feels guilty seems more mundane it is caused by his devotion to his art. It is noticeable that in his fiction from the 1990s and early 2000s, the central characters' adult children are estranged from their parents and positively hostile to their pet projects.

There are some family stories connected with wider history that are certainly worth recording, as he now reveals. When he wrote his famous open letter to Anna Seghers on 14 August 1961 after the Berlin Wall began to be built, Anna Grass was ready to take their three young children to the safety of her parents' house in Switzerland, fearful that the Third World War was about to start. Ute, meanwhile, succeeded in fleeing from East to West Germany, with a fake Swedish passport and the assistance of an Italian dentist. Using Marie's old camera, one of the children imagines that their father could have been waiting at Checkpoint Charlie to greet her.

There is also information on his fiction which he knows will find its way into future accounts of his work, such as how he imagined the four mothers of his children and stepchildren (Anna, Veronika, Ingrid and Ute) as the feminist sailors of the New Ilsebill in *The Rat,* or that while researching locations for *Too Far Afield* in Berlin, he took his youngest daughter rowing in the Tiergarten and on the rollercoaster in Treptower Park.

The eight children in *The Box* compete with Grass's past and future biographers with their collective account of his emotional and extramarital love life, mocking the inevitable speculation about his relationship with Marie: were they ever lovers or was she, sixteen years his senior, a mother substitute? They put out alternative versions of the end of his first marriage to that provided by Jürgs. That period and the novel which he wrote during it, *The Flounder,* is nevertheless at the emotional centre of *The Box.*

To extract great art from family life, novelists have to betray their families. John Updike admitted that he sacrificed his to literature.[17] In *Doctor Faustus,* Thomas Mann killed off a child character based on a grandson. Despite their objections to their roles in *The Box,* Grass in fact holds back on the subject of his children. He also goes easy on himself, imagining not only that his offspring forgive him his absences but that they take his side against the 'newspaper johnnies' who have been on his case since *The Plebeians Rehearse the Uprising.* His tone skirts self-righteousness when it comes to his press critics, who were often only playing their roles in his game of self-presentation. Negative reviews were a price he paid for public influence. After all, he could not always publish as 'Artur Knoff '.

In *Grimms' Words,* Grass's commitment to autobiography attenuates further but the result this time is an insightful literary biography of the brothers Grimm. The book mixes an account of how they came to begin work on the national dictionary which bears their name with riffs on individual words and sounds in that dictionary and reminiscences of his own political campaigning.

As he spends roughly four-fifths of his time on the two brothers, mainly Jacob, who outlived the younger Wilhelm, the book is more biography than autobiography, though Grass sees his own interactions with authority to be reflected in those of his subjects, rehearsing episodes from his past in response to a lexical prompt or an incident.

The Vormärz or Biedermeier period, which was characterized by secret police informers and censorship across the 39 dukedoms, cities, principalities and kingdoms which comprised the German Federation, or *Deutscher Bund*, was a fixed point of reference in speeches and essays and in *Too Far Afield*. In *The Tin Drum*, the 1950s are a second Biedermeier because no one is interested in public affairs or addressing the atrocities of the recent past. Instead they retreat into private worlds. The technique of intermeshing two narrative strands from two different centuries is reminiscent of *Too Far Afield*, but instead of Fonty and Fontane we now have Grass himself and the brothers Grimm. Once again, he presents up to 200 years of German history as a continuum, but the structure this time is much looser than in the earlier novel.

Grimms' Words is neither a novel nor a memoir but, according to its subtitle, 'a declaration of love'. The object of that love is the German language, in particular as it is preserved and presented in the multi-volume German Dictionary (*Wörterbuch* or 'Book of Words') which the Grimms initiated and which was finally completed by two teams of philologists based in East and West Germany in 1960. Grass loves the idea that German linguistic research should have united the two halves of Germany after 1945. It is an example of the *kulturnation* in action. He punctuates the narrative of *Grimms' Words* with verse, as he last did in *The Flounder* and *The Rat*, but prose passages on the sound and meanings of words are often more poetic. The book is ordered like a dictionary, proceeding methodically through the German alphabet. At the translators' conference the near unanimous view was that it was untranslatable, but it has since appeared in Dutch and a Finnish version is in preparation. It is his only work of prose not to be translated into English.

The place of the Grimms' dictionary in the national culture is akin to that of Luther's translation of the Bible or the works of Shakespeare in English. It is a compendium of changing usage, ranging across the centuries from Old and Middle High German to the present, surveying the regions and the dialects from north to south and east to west, noting examples of usage in sayings and proverbs, in literary and common speech, and quoting from an outstanding array of print sources. Grass used their findings on croaking toads in *The Call of the Toad*. By writing about them, he is aligning himself with the Grimm brothers and their great linguistic project, placing himself in other words at the centre of the national culture. He had not really done this up to now. When he invoked literary tradition or his own antecedents he tended to present himself as an outsider to the mainstream. He sees overlaps across time in their public roles. Jacob Grimm was elected in 1849 to the Frankfurt Parliament which met in the Paulskirche, where Grass was also invited to give lectures or eulogies (in 1983, for instance, and 1997). Both he and Jacob also lectured in the Akademie der Künste: Jacob in 1860 in memory of his recently deceased brother; Grass for the first time in 1964.

The Grimms first made an entrance into his fiction in *The Flounder*, which is in part a reworking of a fairy tale in their classic collection. They reappeared in *The Rat* as ministers of state for the environment, anxious to protect the German forests, from which – or at least so they liked to pretend – so many of their tales originated. In both novels Grass is interested in fairy tales as a source of an alternative truth. In *Grimms' Words* the German language represents the 'better side' of the nation, which is an idea he also championed in *The Meeting in Telgte*.

Grass rediscovered an interest in the Grimms in the 2000s when he toured with a concert performance alongside Günter 'Baby'

Sommer and Helene Grass, consisting of the chapter 'The Other Truth' from *The Flounder* and a selection from Brentano and Achim von Arnim's *Des Knaben Wunderhorn*, which inspired the Grimms' collection of fairy tales. Both volumes were assertions of Germanic culture during the French occupation – that French versions of many of the tales pre-dated the German did not detain them. After Achim's death in 1831, his widow Bettina, now a mother of seven, began to write herself, achieving fame with a fictionalized account of her encounter with Goethe, *Goethe's Correspondence with a Child* (1835), as well as recognition for social and political activism. Feminist scholars criticized Grass for assigning a background role in *The Flounder* to such a formidable female character, who was moreover the granddaughter of the first woman German novelist of note, Sophie von La Roche;[18] in *Grimms' Words*, Grass belatedly responds by presenting her centre stage.

Does Bettina von Arnim even provide an historical model of fictionalized biography for his present undertaking? Grass mentions her fictional version of her epistolary friendship with the writer Karoline von Günderode, whose tragic early death at her own hand inspired Christa Wolf to imagine a meeting between her and the greatest suicide in German literature, Heinrich von Kleist. Wolf's short novel was published the same year as Grass's own reimagining of literary history and an encounter which never took place, *The Meeting in Telgte*.[19]

Grass begins *Grimms' Words* with the Grimms' dismissal along with five colleagues from Göttingen University in 1837 for protesting against the King of Hanover's suspension of the constitution. Their stand led indirectly to the commission to compile a dictionary and in 1840, after an intervention from Bettina von Arnim, an invitation from the King of Prussia to work in Berlin. Grass thus presents his own activism in a tradition which includes the 'Göttingen Seven'. The Grimms are Germanists after his own heart in more ways than one, but they were ambiguous heroes who sometimes preferred the quiet life to standing up for their principles. No one can be impressed by their behaviour towards the rebel poet Heinrich Hoffmann von Fallersleben, who turned up a few years later at a birthday party, again at Bettina von Arnim's instigation, and got into trouble with the Prussian police when he joined the brothers on the balcony of their apartment and incited a crowd of well-wishers. Von Fallersleben, whose 'Song of the Germans' (better known after the opening line of the second stanza, as 'Deutschland uber alles') set to a patriotic melody by Haydn became the German national anthem in 1922, was forced to leave Berlin. The Grimms publicly distanced themselves from him. They were currying favour with their royal employer and claimed in true Biedermeier style that they just wanted to get on with their work.

The incident inspires the only instance of self-criticism in *Grimms' Words* when Grass recalls how, in 1971, his comments in the *Süddeutsche Zeitung* directed against the dramatist Heiner Kipphardt resulted in the SPD mayor of Munich not renewing the latter's contract at the state theatre. Kipphardt was on the hard left and not a natural ally of the SPD. What angered Grass was that in the programme for a play by Wolf Biermann about the slaying of dragons in the contemporary world, Kipphardt sanctioned the depiction of a number of such monsters from the worlds of business and politics. At the beginning of an era when self-styled urban guerrillas would soon be carrying out kidnappings and assassinations, Grass had a point. When shortly afterwards he and Anna attended a performance of Ibsen's *Peer Gynt* at West Berlin's radical Theater am Halleschen Ufer, the company initially refused to perform in his presence. A spokesman read out a prepared statement. Grass responded by saying their attempt to expel him reminded him of the Weimar Republic, which was the last time in Germany when individuals were singled out for exclusion in such a way. Although in the end he was allowed to stay, the Kipphardt case clearly stayed on his conscience.

The only other time that he expresses unease with Jacob's behaviour is when the latter reacts with an anti-Semitic comment to a hostile review of the first volume of the dictionary by a critic with Jewish heritage called Daniel Sanders. Jacob does this moreover to his publisher Salomon Hirzel, who was obviously Jewish too, as Jacob would surely have noticed had he paused to reflect. Hirzel's family was also Swiss. His company continued to publish the dictionary after his death, but his grandson was obliged to leave Germany in the 1930s, as Grass reports. Should Jacob's anti-Semitic reflex not have prompted soul-searching from Grass? He could have explored his fifty-year association with Reich-Ranicki or addressed criticism of his treatment of Jewish themes, which was expressed from time to time and would be once more in April 2012.[20] He and Reich-Ranicki would go to their graves with unfinished business.

The failure to find a critical perspective from which to review his past actions makes the autobiographical episodes ultimately the less satisfying part of *Grimms' Words*. An enumeration of these episodes, only a tiny proportion of which is new, shows that he sees continuity not just between his own epoch and that of the Grimms but across his own long career in the public eye, from his open letter to Anna Seghers in 1961 to a speech to the PEN conference in 2006. *Grimms' Words* was well received on the whole, opening another late chapter in the German public's increasingly love-and-hate affair with their leading author. There would be a few more such chapters, one being his ill-judged decision to publish 'What Has to Be Said'.

Epilogue: Poetry and Death

Grass died suddenly after catching an infection. He and Ute had been taking a short holiday on the Baltic coast. When Ute phoned to say that she was feeling unwell, Hilke Ohsoling drove out to fetch them both home. The return car journey on 11 April 2015 was joyous, the weather bright. Grass, the eternal passenger who never learned to drive, took pleasure in looking out of the window at places he still wanted to visit, but once in Behlendorf, Ute's bug passed to him. Despite a transfer to hospital, he died early in the morning of Monday 13 April. To the end he was writing in a standing position at his chest-high desk and working in his studio, having corrected proofs of his last manuscript the previous week. His last public appearance was the premiere of another adaptation of *The Tin Drum* at Hamburg's Thalia Theater just the week before that. Günter Grass did not retire.

His death predictably made news bulletins across the world and headlines in Germany. The literary website *perlentaucher.de* reported that the tone of the German obituaries was 'cool'. August 2015 saw the publication of the valedictory *Of All That Ends*, as planned, on the subjects of death and decrepitude, last memories and favourite pastimes, the joy of writing and the perilous state of the world. Grass picks up some familiar themes for one last time. He writes about old and new technologies (the wonders of the Olivetti portable typewriter and the dangers of total surveillance in the digital age), about pills, ailments and failing body parts.

Yet in documenting approaching death, the book asserts life. The lyrical 'I' and first-person narrator show a determination to express himself to the end and in ways not previously tried out. For the first time poems alternate with short prose and both are interspersed with sketches illustrating and supplementing the written texts. They depict falling autumn leaves and coffin nails, windfalls and feathers, tobacco pipes (deadly for his lungs but essential for his art), dead birds and dried-out frogs' skins, a self-portrait without his dentures bearing his last natural tooth, which is the subject of both verse and prose entries, or the rounded outlines of a woman's torso which follows a paean to the female body in all its remembered plenitude and variety. The pencil sketches are in black and white after the coloured ink drawings in *Mayflies* from 2012, which was also on transient subjects – a mayfly exists as a larva for several years but lives only for a day as a winged insect. Grass's switch to colour in *Lost and Found Items for Non-readers* in 1997 indicated a change in mood after he made his peace with unification, which he sustained through most of his remaining publications. The exceptions are *Last Dances*, which was about fading powers and last pleasures, and *The Box*, which celebrated the art of the black-and-white photograph. The switch back to black and white is determined by the presence of death at his shoulder.

There turns out to be a narrative architecture to *Of All That Ends*. It starts in the autumn and goes through winter and spring to summer and approaching autumn again – the centenary of the First World War identifies the year as 2014. Death will come, but until it does Grass will squeeze out life's last drop of black ink, as he reports dreaming of doing in 'Sepia Nature'. Milking a squid for its ink, he imagines, is like making love to a water sprite. The image combines sex with food and writing, sustenance for the three hungers which have driven his life. The underwater dream is the third in the series of 97 verse or prose pieces which concludes with the title poem in the Danzig dialect of his youth: 'Vonne Endlichkait' (Of All That

Ends). Danzig German will survive only as long as the last Danziger. For one last year Grass will carry on writing about the passing of the seasons, cooking mushrooms found in the woods, drawing inspiration from authors whose books he has read throughout his career, such as Rabelais and Jean Paul; he will follow the news of the war in Syria, the economic crisis in Greece, be reminded of his Langfuhr grandfather the carpenter, the model for Liebenau's father in *Dog Years*, who died believing the politicians – convinced that he would return home one day soon to find everything in his workshop just as he had left it.

At the centre of the collection is the longest narrative, 'In What and Where We Will Lie', a macabre comedy recounting how he and Ute order their coffins from a local carpenter – his in birch, hers in pine, both with four cloth handles on either side, one for each of their eight children to carry them to their graves. The carpenter has previously made bookshelves and writing desks for the elderly couple and stays for a glass of fruit schnapps after he takes this last order and once again a few weeks later when he delivers the finished products. Grass tries out his coffin, which fits him perfectly, and Ute regrets not taking his picture as he looked so peaceful. He decides that he will ask to have it lined with leaves when the time comes. The coffins take up residence in the cellar and Ute uses hers to store two dozen dahlia bulbs, ready to plant in the spring. Then in mid-winter, as they are watching a late-night French thriller on TV, they suffer a break-in and the coffins, including the dahlia bulbs, are stolen. Towards the end of the volume, once spring has come, he reports that just as mysteriously the coffins are returned but minus the bulbs. His last tooth falls out shortly afterwards too.

In private correspondence, Grass often announced that he was taking pleasure in returning to practise a particular art form, such as sculpture in the early 1980s or watercolours in 1995 after the furore which greeted *Too Far Afield*. He also enjoyed the activity of writing but the happiness it could afford was momentary, as he confided to the literary critic Heinz Ludwig Arnold halfway through that novel:

> Most colleagues whom I know or believe I know claim that they hate writing and talk about it as an ordeal they put themselves through, but I have always taken pleasure from it as a challenge which I take seriously. But if you asked me about moments of happiness, I could only point to a winding sentence which has been well formulated or a chapter successfully concluded.[1]

It is for these well-turned sentences and rounded chapters that he should be remembered.[1]

References

Prologue

1 Thomas Mann, 'Von deutscher Republik. Gerhart Hauptmann zum sechzigsten Geburtstag', *Essays*, vol. II: *Politische Reden und Schriften*, ed. Hermann Kurzke (Frankfurt, 1977), pp. 59–93. Whitman wrote: 'For you these from me, O Democracy, to serve you ma femme! For you, for you I am trilling these songs.'

2 John Irving's Eulogy for Günter Grass, *The Globe and Mail* (11 May 2015).

3 As 'Das Spielzeug aus der Welt genommen', *Süddeutsche Zeitung* (11 May 2015).

4 Willy Brandt, *North-South, a Programme for Survival: Report of the Independent Commission on International Development Issues* (London, 1980).

5 See Hans Werner Richter, *Im Etablissement der Schmetterlinge. Einundzwanzig Portraits aus der Gruppe 47* (Munich/Vienna, 1986), p. 123.

6 *Der Unbequeme. Der Dichter Günter Grass*, dirs Nadja Frenz and Sigrun Matthiesen, 2007.

7 Volker Neuhaus, *Schreiben gegen die verstreichende Zeit. Zu Leben und Werk von Günter Grass* (Munich, 1997); Michael Jürgs, *Bürger Grass. Biografie eines deutschen Dichters* (Munich, 2002); Volker Neuhaus, *Günter Grass. Eine Biographie: Schriftsteller, Künstler, Zeitgenosse* (Göttingen, 2012).

8 Harro Zimmermann, *Günter Grass und die Deutschen: Eine Entwirrung* (Göttingen, 2017).

9 *Der Fall Fonty. 'Ein weites Feld' von Günter Grass im Spiegel der Kritik*, ed. Oskar Negt and Daniela Hermes (Göttingen, 1996).

10 *Zeit sich einzumischen. Die Kontroverse um Günter Grass und die Laudatio auf Yaşar Kemal in der Paulskirche*, ed. Manfred Bissinger and Daniela Hermes (Göttingen, 1998).

11 *Ein Buch, ein Bekenntnis. Die Debatte um Günter Grass' 'Beim Häuten der Zwiebel"*, ed. Martin Kölbel (Göttingen, 2007); *Was gesagt wurde. Eine Dokumentation über Günter Grass' 'Was gesagt werden muss' und die deutsche Debatte*, ed. Heinrich Detering and Per Øhrgaard (Göttingen, 2013).

12 Harro Zimmermann, *Günter Grass unter den Deutschen. Chronik eines Verhältnisses* (Göttingen, 2006/2010).

13 Timm Niklas Pietsch, *'Wer hört noch zu?' Günter Grass als politischer Redner und Essayist* (Essen, 2006).

14 *The Etchings* (vol. I), *The Lithographs* (vol. II), ed. Hilke Ohsoling (Göttingen, 2007).

15 Kai Schlüter, *Günter Grass im Visier. Die Stasi-Akte. Eine Dokumentation mit Kommentaren von Günter Grass und Zeitzeugen* (Berlin, 2010).

16 *Willy Brandt und Günter Grass. Der Briefwechsel*, ed. Martin Kölbel (Göttingen, 2013).

1 From Danzig to Paris, 1927–59: Living *The Tin Drum*

1 Peter Oliver Loew, *Danzig. Biographie einer Stadt* (Munich, 2011), p. 24.

2 'No Wonder' in Manheim's translation.

3 Hermann Kurzke, 'Der Mythos als Ruine. *Die Blechtrommel* nach dem vierfachen Schrisftsinn gedeutet', in *Ein Buch schreibt Geschichte. 50 Jahre 'Die Blechtrommel'*, ed. Jörg-Philipp Thomsa (Lübeck, 2009), pp. 83–92.

4 Dieter Stolz, 'Nomen est omen. *Ein weites Feld* by Günter Grass', in *'Whose Story?': Continuities in Contemporary German-language Literature*, ed. Arthur Williams, Stuart Parkes and Julian Preece (Oxford, 1998), pp. 149–6, esp. p. 155.

5 Günter Grass, *Atelier des métamorphoses. Entretiens avec Nicole Casanova* (Paris, 1979), pp. 26–7.

6 *Die Box* (Göttingen, 2008), p. 106.

7 Heinrich Vormweg, *Günter Grass in Selbstzeugnissen und Bilddokumenten* (Reinbek bei Hamburg, 1986), p. 22.

8 As he recalls in a letter to Gerhard Steidl, 22 October 1997.

9 Grass to Eduard Reifferscheid, 27 August 1979.

10 Grass to Reifferscheid, 25 January 1978.

11 Grass, *Atelier des métamorphoses*, p. 18.

12 Michael Minden points out that 'Three rapes mark out the architectonic shape of the book: that perpetrated by the Goth in "Woran ich mich nicht erinnern will", that committed by Axel on Agnes in the fourth month, and the multiple rape suffered by Sibylle in the eighth'; 'Implications of the Narrative Technique in *Der Butt*', in *Günter Grass's Der Butt: Sexual Politics and the Male Myth of History*, ed. Philip Brady, Timothy McFarland and John J. White (Oxford, 1990), pp. 187–202, here p. 194.

13 Renée Fülop-Müller, *Der heilige Teufel. Rasputin und die Frauen* (1927) was a best-seller between the wars.

14 Barker Fairley, *Wilhelm Raabe: An Introduction to his Novels* (Oxford, 1961), pp. 172–3.

15 Grass, *Atelier des métamorphoses*, p. 21.

16 Grass to Hans Bender, 25 February 1970.

17 'Erinnerungen an Danzig. Günter Grass im Gespräch mit Ekkehart Rudolph', 4 August 1990, Süddeutscher Rundfunk.

18 'Der Lernende Lehrer. Rede auf einem Gesamtschul-Kongreß' (May 1999), xii:532–50, here p. 533.

19 Grass to Figes, 30 October 1980.

20 Quoted by Anne Fuchs, *Phantoms of War in Contemporary German Literature, Film, and Discourse: The Politics of Memory* (Rochester, NY, 2008), p. 164.

21 Though Malte Herwig's title promises more than his book delivers: *Die Flakhelfer. Wie aus Hitlers jüngsten Parteimitgliedern Deutschlands führende Demokraten wurden* (Munich, 2013).

22 'Rede von der Gewöhnung', xi:225–38, here p. 231.

23 Volker Neuhaus, *Schreiben gegen die verstreichende Zeit. Zu Leben und Werk von Günter Grass* (Munich, 1997), p. 28.

24 Quoted by Vormweg, *Günter Grass in Selbstzeugnissen und Bilddokumenten*, p. 15.

25 See also Dieter Stolz, 'Mein Grass – ein ganz persönlicher Erfahrungsbericht', *Freipass. Schriften der Günter und Ute Grass Stiftung* (2014) vol. i, pp. 113–36, esp. p. 118.

26 In conversation at the Grass Haus, Lübeck, 11 February 2016.

27 Salman Rushdie in an introduction to Grass's Essays (1984), reprinted in *Imaginary Homelands: Essays and Criticism, 1981–1991* (London, 1992), pp. 276–81, esp. p. 279.

28 Grass, *Atelier des métamorphoses*, p. 37.

29 Günter Grass and Harro Zimmermann, *Vom Abenteuer der Aufklärung* (Göttingen, 1999), p. 64.

30 Albert Camus, *Der Mensch in der Revolte* [L'homme revolté, 1951], trans. Justus Streller (Reinbek bei Hamburg, 1953). See also *Der Mythos von Sisyphos. Ein Versuch über das Absurde* [Le mythe de Sisyphe, 1942], trans. Hans Georg Brenner and Wolfdietrich Rasch (Düsseldorf, 1950).

31 Albert Camus, *The Rebel*, trans. Anthony Bower (Harmondsworth, 1971).

32 See Arno Barnert, 'Eine "herzgraue" Freundschaft. Der Briefwechsel zwischen Paul Celan und Günter Grass', *Textkritische Beiträge*, 9 (2004), pp. 65–127.

33 Celan's extensive private library is now in the Deutsches Literaturarchiv, Marbach.

34 Grass, *Atelier des métamorphoses*, pp. 46–7.

35 *Celan Handbuch. Leben, Werk, Wirkung*, ed. Markus May, Peter Goßens and Jürgen Lehmann (Stuttgart, 2008), p. 363.

36 Sabine Richter, 'Das Kaleidoskop des Günter Grass. Jüdische Karikaturen aus der Kaschubei', in *Das literarische und kulturelle Erbe von Danzig und Gdańsk*, ed. Andrzej Katny (Frankfurt, 2004), pp. 47–53.

37 Erwin Lichtenstein, *Die Juden der Freien Stadt Danzig unter der Herrschaft des Nationalsozialismus, 1933–1945* (Tübingen, 1973).

38 Ruth K. Angress, '*Der Butt*: A Feminist Perspective', in *Adventures of a Flounder: Critical Essays on Günter Grass's 'Der Butt'*, ed. Gertrud Bauer Pickar (Munich, 1982), pp. 43–50.

39 Ruth K. Angress, 'A "Jewish Problem" in German Postwar Fiction', *Modern Judaism*, V/3 (1985), pp. 215–33. The title of the German version of the article, which appeared the following year, is phrased as a question: 'Gibt es ein "Judenproblem" in der deutschen Nachkriegsliteratur?' reprinted in *Katastrophen. Über deutsche Literatur* (Göttingen, 1994), pp. 9–38.

40 Survey quoted by Siegfried Mews, *Günter Grass and His Critics: From 'The Tin Drum' to 'Crabwalk'* (Rochester, NY, 2008), pp. 2–3.

41 Marcel Reich-Ranicki, *Günter Grass. Aufsätze* (Zurich, 1992), pp. 13–18 ('Auf gut Glück getrommelt', 1960) and pp. 21–8 ('Selbstkritik des "Blechtrommel"-Kritikers', 1963).

42 Marcel Reich-Ranicki, *Mein Leben* (Stuttgart, 1999), p. 11.

43 Ibid., p. 460.

44 Ibid., p. 293.

2 Art and Violence in the Early Fiction

1 See Stuart Taberner, *Aging and Old-age Style in Günter Grass, Ruth Klüger, Christa Wolf, and Martin Walser: The Mannerism of a Late Period* (Rochester, NY, 2013), esp. p. 43.

2 See Klaus von Schilling, *Schuldmotoren. Artistisches Erzählen in Günter Grass' Danziger Trilogie* (Bielefeld, 2002).

3 Max Frisch, *Die Tagebücher* (Frankfurt, 1978), pp. 714–15.

4 Hans Magnus Enzensberger entitled his famous review, 'Wilhelm Meister, auf Blech getrommelt', reprinted in *Von Buch zu Buch. Günter Grass in der Kritik*, ed. Gert Loschütz (Darmstadt, 1968), pp. 8–12.

5 Quoted by Volker Neuhaus, *Günter Grass* (Stuttgart, 2010), p. 26.

6 S. S. Prawer, 'The Death of Sigismund Markus: The Jews of Danzig in the Fiction of Günter Grass', in *Danzig, between East and West: Aspects of Modern Jewish History*, ed. Isadore Twersky (Cambridge, MA, 1985), pp. 95–108.

7 In conversation at the first 'Lange Nacht für Günter Grass', Grass Haus, Lübeck, 13 April 2016.

8 'Der lernende Lehrer' (1999), XX:40–58, p. 49.

9 Enno Stahl, *Für die Katz und wider die Maus. Pohlands Film nach Grass* (Berlin, 2012).

10 Grass to Malte Herwig in 2011, quoted in Herwig, *Die Flakhelfer. Wie aus Hitlers jüngsten Parteimitgliedern Deutschlands führende Demokraten wurden* (Munich, 2013), p. 232. See also Günter Grass, *Atelier des métamorphoses. Entretiens avec Nicole Casanova* (Paris, 1979), p. 64.

11 'Schreiben nach Auschwitz' (1990) (XII:239–61, esp. p. 254).

12 Michael Minden, '"Grass auseinandergeschrieben": Günter Grass's *Hundejahre* and Mimesis', *German Quarterly*, LXXXVI/1 (2013), pp. 25–42, here p. 27.

13 Salman Rushdie, *Imaginary Homelands: Essays and Criticism, 1981–1991* (London, 1992), p. 277.

14 See Dorothee Römhild, '"Der Hund ist scharf und hält sicher nicht sehr viel von Künstlern": Zur kynozentrischen Poetologie der *Hundejahre* im Spannungsfeld von Ontologie und Ästhetik', in *Von Katz und Maus und mea. culpa. Religiöse Motive im Werk von Günter Grass*, ed. Anselm Weyer and Volker Neuhaus (Frankfurt, 2013), pp. 35–48, esp. pp. 40–41.

15 As recorded on the short documentary film, *Spätschicht. Günter Grass bei der Arbeit an Radierungen zu Hundejahre*, dir. Sigrun Matthiesen, 2013.

16 *Ein Buch schreibt Geschichte: 50 Jahre 'Die Blechtrommel'*, ed. Jörg-Philipp Thomsa (Lübeck, 2009).

17 Captured on *Der Unbequeme. Der Dichter Günter Grass*, dirs Nadja Frenz and Sigrun Matthiesen, 2007.

18 Kurt Lothar Tank, *Günter Grass* (Berlin, 1965), p. 80.

19 Quoted by John Wieczorek, *Between Sarmatia and Socialism: The Life and Works of Johannes Bobrowski* (Amsterdam, 1999), p. 175.

20 Johannes Bobrowski, *Levins Mühle* (Frankfurt, 1964).

21 Edgar Hilsenrath, *Der Nazi und der Friseur* (Cologne, 1977); first published in English translation, 1971.

22 Grass to Reifferscheid, 19 May 1969.

23 See Ulrich Enzensberger, *Die Jahre der Kommune 1. Berlin, 1967–1969* (Cologne, 2004), p. 123 and pp. 184–5.

24 Volker Neuhaus, '"Was sich ablagert". Nachwort zu *örtlich betäubt*', in *Werkausgabe in zehn Bänden*, ed. Neuhaus (Darmstadt/Neuwied, 1987), vol. IV, p. 574.

3 Public Uses of Fame: Willy Brandt and the SPD

1 Kurt Lothar Tank, *Günter Grass* (Berlin, 1965), p. 11.

2 Heinrich Vormweg, *Günter Grass in Selbstzeugnissen und Bilddokumenten* (Reinbek bei Hamburg, 1986), p. 8.

3 Volker Neuhaus, *Schreiben gegen die verstreichende Zeit. Zu Leben und Werk von Günter Grass* (Munich, 1997), pp. 94–102.

4 Inside cover blurb, Volker Neuhaus, *Günter Grass. Eine Biographie: Schriftsteller, Künstler, Zeitgenosse* (Göttingen, 2012).

5 Michael Jürgs, *Bürger Grass. Biografie eines deutschen Dichters* (Munich, 2002), p. 254.

6 Harro Zimmermann, *Günter Grass unter den Deutschen. Chronik eines Verhältnisses* (Göttingen, 2006/2010), pp. 378 and 401.

7 *Willy Brandt und Günter Grass. Der Briefwechsel*, ed. Martin Kölbel (Göttingen, 2013), p. 891.

8 Ibid., pp. 659–61.

9 Hans Werner Richter, *Im Etablissement der Schmetterlinge. Einundzwanzig Portraits aus der Gruppe 47* (Munich/Vienna, 1986), pp. 127–8.

10 *Steine Wälzen. Essays und Reden* (Göttingen, 2007), with an afterword by Oskar Negt.

11 *Die Alternative oder brauchen wir eine neue Regierung?* (Reinbek bei Hamburg, 1961), ed. Martin Walser, was published in August with a total print run of 75,000.

12 Kai Schlüter, *Günter Grass im Visier. Die Stasi-Akte. Eine Dokumentation mit Kommentaren von Günter Grass und Zeitzeugen* (Berlin, 2010), p. 75.

13 See *Was würde Bebel dazu sagen? Zur aktuellen Lage der Sozialdemokratie*, ed. Manfred Bissinger and Wolfgang Thierse (Göttingen, 2013).

14 See Uwe Johnson, Anna Grass and Günter Grass, *Der Briefwechsel*, ed. Arno Barnert (Frankfurt, 2007), pp. 197–9.

15 See 'Einleitung', *Günter Grass. Stimmen aus dem Leseland*, ed. Klaus Pezold (Leipzig, 2003), pp. 19–48.

16 Brandt to Grass, *Briefwechsel*, ed. Kölbel, 10 July 1977, p. 675.

17 Kurt Sontheimer, *Thomas Mann und die Deutschen* and *Antidemokratisches Verhalten in der Weimarer Republik* (both Munich, 1961 and 1962).

18 'In Sachen Bremer Literaturpreis', in *Günter Grass. Dokumente zur politischen Wirkung*, ed. Heinz Ludwig Arnold and Franz Josef Görtz (Munich, 1971), pp. 265–81, here p. 270.

19 Kurt Wolff to Grass, 14 January 1960 in Günter Grass/Helen Wolff, *Briefe, 1959–1994*, ed. Daniela Hermes (Göttingen, 2003), p. 14.

20 See Volker Hentschel, *Ludwig Erhard. Ein Politikerleben* (Munich, 1996), pp. 572–3.

21 Anna Grass to Johnson, 23 May 1968 in *Briefwechsel*, ed. Barnert, p. 127.

22 Grass to Egon Bahr, 24 June 1968.

23 Grass to Brandt, 3 October 1969, in *Briefwechsel*, ed. Kölbel, pp. 309–13.

24 Brandt to Grass, 12 December 1969, ibid., pp. 328–9.

25 Grass to Brandt, 15 May 1979, ibid., p. 695.

26 Max Frisch, *Die Tagebucher, 1966–1971* (Frankfurt, 1972), pp. 714–23.

27 Max Frisch, *Aus dem Berliner Journal*, ed. Thomas Strässle with Margit Unser (Frankfurt, 2014), pp. 158–60. The editors are wrong to state that Grass's dissatisfaction with Brandt's performance as chancellor can be attributed to his failure to secure a ministerial role (p. 229).

28 *Günter Grass auf Tour für Willy Brandt. Die legendäre Wahlkampfreise 1969*, ed. Kai Schlüter (Berlin, 2011).

4 Back to the Future, Forward to the Past

1 Dieter Stolz, *Vom privaten Motivkomplex zum epischen Weltentwurf* (Würzburg, 1994).

2 Susanne Schädlich, *Immer wieder Dezember. Der Westen, die Stasi, der Onkel und ich* (Munich, 2009), p. 37.

3 Grass to Wolff, 6 June 1984, in Günter Grass/Helen Wolff, *Briefe, 1959–1994*, ed. Daniela Hermes (Göttingen, 2003), pp. 321–2.

4 See Helen Finch, 'Günter Grass and Gender', *The Cambridge Companion to Günter Grass*, ed. Stuart Taberner (Cambridge, 2009), pp. 81–95.

5 Such as Werner Frizen, who has edited *Der Butt* for the new complete edition scheduled to appear in 2019 (Göttingen).

6 Grass to Figes, 31 January 1977.

7 Grass to Hildesheimer, 16 May 1977.

8 Grass to Figes, 31 January 1977; Grass to Hildesheimer, 22 August 1977.

9 Gisela Schneider, *'Über das Essen, den Nachgeschmack'. Studien zum Motiv des Essens in ausgewählten Werken von Günter Grass*, PhD thesis, National University of Ireland, Cork.

10 Marcel Reich-Ranicki, 'Ein Buttessen mit Folgen' (2002), in *Unser Grass* (Munich, 2003), pp. 183–7.

11 *Sechs Jahrzehnte*, p. 48.

12 Quoted by Volker Neuhaus, *Schreiben gegen die verstreichende Zeit. Zu Leben und Werk von Günter Grass* (Munich, 1997), p. 88.

13 Andrzej Fac, 'Die Wahlbekanntschaften'/'Faca Grass – Grass Fac', in *Von Danzig nach Lübeck. Günter Grass und Polen/Z Gdańska do Lubeki*.

Günter Grass i Polska, ed. Jörg-Philipp-Thomsa and Viktoria Krason (Lübeck/Gdańsk, 2010), pp. 67–77.

14 *Teure Vergangenheit* was broadcast by Norddeutscher Rundfunk in December 1975.

15 Paul Simson, *Geschichte der Stadt Danzig*, 4 vols, vol. 1: *Von den Anfängen bis 1517* (Danzig, 1913), pp. 290–95.

16 Nicole Casanova, *Mes Allemagnes* (Paris, 1987), pp. 133–40. See also Osman Durrani, *Fictions of Germany: Images of the German Nation in the Modern Novel* (Edinburgh, 1994), pp. 134–81.

17 August Bebel, *Die Frau und der Sozialismus* (1879), reissued and revised more than fifty times in the author's lifetime.

18 Eva Figes, *Patriarchal Attitudes* (London, 1978), p. 35. In *Of All That Ends* (2015), Grass, however, credits Claude Lévi-Strauss, *The Raw and the Cooked* (first published as *Le Cru et le cuit*, 1964) for providing him with this idea. As the book appeared in English translation in 1969 and German in 1971, it could have been their common source.

19 Eva Figes, 'Grass Roots: An Interview with Günter Grass, the German Writer and Politician', *The Guardian* (12 November 1965).

20 Eva Figes, 'Habits of the Under Toad . . . and *The Flounder*', *Observer* (15 October 1978). The first part is a review of John Irving's *The World According to Garp*.

21 See Peter Rühmkorf, *Die Jahre die Ihr kennt. Anfälle und Erinnerungen* (Hamburg, 1972), pp. 133–4, and Klaus Rainer Röhl, *Die Genossin* (Vienna, 1975), pp. 187–8. Both hint strongly that Grass and Meinhof had an affair.

22 See Julia Baudisch, '"Und auch Ilsebill war von Anfang an da". Der schönste erste Satz in der Prosa Günter Grass', *Berliner Hefte zur Geschichte des literarischen Lebens* (2013), vol. x, pp. 128–45.

23 Grass to Figes, 31 January 1984.

24 Grass to Albrecht Schöne, 6 June 1975.

25 Grass to Martin Gregor-Dellin, 8 June 1984.

26 Rebecca Braun, *Constructing Authorship in the Work of Günter Grass* (Oxford, 2008), pp. 12–38.

27 See Helmut Böttiger, *Die Gruppe 47. Als die deutsche Literatur Geschichte schrieb* (Munich, 2012), pp. 122–56, who quashes this particular canard.

28 Jörg Magenau appears to have been directly inspired by Grass in his
    factual account of the penultimate meeting of the Gruppe: *Princeton
    66. Die abenteuerliche Reise der Gruppe 47* (Stuttgart, 2015).
29 For example, Klaus Haberkamm, 'Verspäteter Grimmelshausen aus
    der Kaschubei. Verspätete Utopie? Simplicianisches in Grass' *Der Butt*',
    Simpliciana. Schriften der Grimmelshausen-Gesellschaft 6/7 (1985),
    pp. 123–38.
30 Albrecht Schöne, ed., *Das Zeitalter des Barock. Texte und Zeugnisse*
    (Munich, 1963) and *Kürbishütte und Königsberg. Modellversuch einer
    sozialgeschichtlichen Entzifferung poetischer Texte am Bespiel Simon
    Dach* (Munich, 1975).
31 Grass to Ralph Manheim, 27 November 1964.
32 Grass to Hildesheimer, 16 May 1977.
33 Alexander Weber, 'J. M. Schneuber. Der Ich-Erzähler in Günter Grass',
    Das Treffen in Telgte', *Daphnis*, 15 (1986), pp. 95–122.
34 Grass to Brandt, 15 December 1978, *Willy Brandt und Günter Grass.
    Der Briefwechsel*, ed. Martin Kölbel (Göttingen, 2013), pp. 686–91.
    See Günter Grass, *Atelier des métamorphoses. Entretiens avec Nicole
    Casanova* (Paris, 1979), pp. 90–91.
35 Quoted by Schädlich, *Immer wieder Dezember*, p. 56.
36 See Kai Schlüter, *Günter Grass im Visier. Die Stasi-Akte. Eine
    Dokumentation mit Kommentaren von Günter Grass und Zeitzeugen*
    (Berlin, 2010), pp. 71–178, and Schädlich, *Immer wieder Dezember*,
    pp. 54–69.
37 Schädlich, *Immer Wieder Dezember*, p. 63.
38 According to the writer F. C. Delius, for example, in conversation
    at the Literaturforum im Brecht Haus, Berlin, 4 July 2016.

5 Crying Wolf in 'Orwell's Decade'?

1 Grass to Tom Rosenthal, 11 August 1981.
2 Grass to Figes, 30 October 1980.
3 As I did at an event at the Jacobs University, Bremen, in October 2007.
4 Quoted by Harro Zimmermann, *Günter Grass unter den Deutschen.
   Chronik eines Verhältnisses* (Göttingen, 2006/2010), p. 421.
5 Ibid., p. 423.

6   According to the civil rights activist and post-Wende critic of
    reunification, Daniela Dahn, in *Gunter Grass: Stimmen aus dem
    Leseland*, ed. Klaus Pezold (Leipzig, 2003), p. 9.

7   Wolff to Grass, 15 December 1982, Günter Grass/Helen Wolff,
    Briefe, 1959–1994, ed. Daniela Hermes (Göttingen, 2003),
    pp. 302–5.

8   Grass to Figes, 4 October 1985.

9   Grass to Wolff, 1 July 1985, *Briefe, 1959–1994*, p. 336.

10 Quoted in 'Le nouveau roman de Günter Grass. Eva Figes a rencontré
    le romancier allemand à Hambourg', *Le Monde* (7 March 1986).

11 Günter Ratte, *Der Grass* (Frankfurt, 1986), p. 20.

12 *Per Anhalter durch die Galaxis*, tr. Benjamin Schwarz (Munich, 1981).
    In *Der Grass*, there is an 'interpreter fish' 'which we have borrowed
    from Douglas Adams', p. 23.

13 Grass to Hans Altenhein, 28 February 1985.

14 Grass to Wolff, 3 June 1986, *Briefe, 1959–1994*, p. 343.

15 Ilija Trojanow, 'Auf den Spuren von Günter Grass. Zungen zeigen
    in Kalkutta', in *Der Sadhu an der Teufelswand. Reportagen aus einem
    anderen Indien* (Munich, 2001), pp. 152–60, here p. 160.

16 'Lieber Pfeifenonkel', *Der Spiegel* (12 January 1987).

17 Kai Schlüter, *Günter Grass im Visier. Die Stasi-Akte. Eine Dokumentation
    mit Kommentaren von Günter Grass und Zeitzeugen* (Berlin, 2010),
    pp. 257–94.

18 *Grimms Wörter*, pp. 341–6.

19 For example, in Grass and Pavel Kohout, *Briefe über die Grenze. Versuche
    eines Ost-West Dialoges* (Berlin, 1968), p. 47.

20 'Viel Gefühl, wenig Bewußtsein', *Der Spiegel* (20 November 1989).

21 'Lastenausgleich', *Frankfurter Rundschau* (19 December 1989).

22 *Deutscher Lastenausgleich. Wider das dumpfe Einheitsgebot. Reden und
    Gespräche* (Neuwied, 1990).

23 'Kurze Rede eines vaterlandslosen Gesellen', *Die Zeit* (9 February 1990);
    'Schreiben nach Auschwitz', *Die Zeit* (23 February 1990).

24 Grass to Ibrahim Böhme, 5 February 1990.

25 Dahn, *Stimmen aus dem Leserland*, p. 39.

26 See 'Der Zug ist abgefahren – aber wohin? Offener Brief an Rudolf
    Augstein', *Die Tageszeitung* (23 February 1990).

27 Grass to Wolff, 17 April 1991, *Briefe, 1959–1994*, p. 377.

28 See the entry 'Unkenrufe' (added around 1920) in the *Deutsches Wörterbuch*, begun by Jacob and Wilhelm Grimm in 1852 and completed in 1960.

29 Grass to Oskar Negt, 10 September 1992.

30 Grass to Bahr, 10 September 1990.

6 Learning to Love the Berlin Republic: *Too Far Afield*

1 Johann Wolfgang von Goethe and Friedrich Schiller, 'Über epische und dramatische Dichtung' (1797).

2 Gespräch mit Günter Grass zur Problematik der Feiern zum 100. Jahrestag der Reichsgründung, 18 January 1971, Westdeutscher Rundfunk.

3 See Hans Joachim Schädlich, *Zwischen Schauplatz und Elfenbeinturm* (Göttingen, 2001), esp. the second essay 'Tallhover – ein weites Feld. Autobiographische Notiz', pp. 25–38, here p. 26 (first published in 1998).

4 *Unterwegs von Deutschland nach Deutschland. Tagebuch 1990* (Göttingen, 2009), pp. 249–51.

5 See Roland Berbig, 'Das neuste Material in Sachen "Fontane". Dieter Stolz' Korrespondenz mit Günter Grass', *Berliner Hefte zur Geschichte des literarischen Lebens* (2013), vol. x, pp. 83–125.

6 'Ein Schlachtfeld', part of the cycle entitled 'Die Albigenser', Nikolaus Lenau, *Sämtliche Werke und Briefe*, 2 vols, vol. i: *Gedichte und Versepen* (Frankfurt, 1971), p. 834.

7 Dieter Stolz, 'Nomen est omen. *Ein weites Feld* by Günter Grass', in Arthur Williams, '*Whose Story?': Continuities in Contemporary German-language Literature*, ed. Stuart Parkes and Julian Preece (Oxford, 1998), pp. 154–5.

8 'Der lesende Arbeiter' (1974), xi:921–31.

9 Interview in *Text und Kritik*, ed. Heinz Ludwig Arnold (1978), p. 5.

10 Per Øhrgaard, *Günter Grass. Ein Deutscher Schriftsteller wird besichtigt*, trans. Christoph Bartmann (Munich and Vienna, 2005), p. 158.

11 The title of an anthology of reviews and articles about the novel which appeared in the press on publication: *Der Fall Fonty. 'Ein weites Feld'*

von Günter Grass im Spiegel der Kritik, ed. Oskar Negt and Daniela Hermes (Göttingen, 1996).

12 Günter Grass and Harro Zimmermann, *Vom Abenteuer der Aufklärung* (Göttingen, 1999), p. 234.

13 'Öffentliche Hinrichtung der Christa Wolf', *Frankfurter Rundschau* (14 December 2011).

14 Wolfgang Schorlau, *Die blaue Liste. Denglers erster Fall* (Cologne, 2003).

15 Grass and Zimmermann, *Vom Abenteuer der Aufklärung*, p. 248.

16 See 'Rede gegen die Gewöhnung', xiv:770–78, and Michael Jürgs, *Bürger Grass. Biografie eines deutschen Dichters* (Munich, 2002), pp. 264–5.

17 Hans Joachim Schädlich, *Aktenkundig*. Mit Beiträgen von Wolf Biermann, Jürgen Fuchs, Joachim Gauck, Lutz Rathenow, Vera Wollenberger (Reinbek bei Hamburg, 1992).

18 All details from Schädlich, *Zwischen Schauplatz und Elfenbeinturm*.

19 Monika Maron, 'Die Unke hat geirrt', *Süddeutsche Zeitung* (7 September 2009).

20 See the title essay in *Zwischen Schauplatz und Elfenbeinturm*.

21 Kai Schlüter, *Günter Grass im Visier. Die Stasi-Akte. Eine Dokumentation mit Kommentaren von Günter Grass und Zeitzeugen* (Berlin, 2010), pp. 104–6. See also Marian Blasberg, 'Der Dandy von Ost-Berlin', *Die Zeit* (31 December 2008).

7 The New Nation Is Me

1 Grass to Peter Glotz, 17 February 1994.

2 Published in English by Oxford University Press in 2007, 2 vols, trans. Alexander J. Sager.

3 Grass to Gerhard Schröder, 7 May 1998.

4 *Zeit sich einzumischen. Die Kontroverse um Günter Grass und die Laudatio auf Yaşar Kemal in der Paulskirche*, ed. Manfred Bissinger and Daniela Hermes (Göttingen, 1998), p. 34.

5 'Rede über den Standort' (1997), xii:471–90 and 'Freiheit nach Börsenmaß' (2005), xii:693–701.

6 Günter Grass, Daniela Dahn and Johano Strasser, eds, *In einem reichen Land. Zeugnisse alltäglichen Leidens an der Gesellschaft* (Göttingen, 2002), p. 15.

7 See Gerhard Schröder, *Was kommt, was bleibt. Ein Porträt in Gedanken und Zitaten. Mit nachträglichen Gedanken von Günter Grass und Illustrationen von Martin Wember*, ed. Detlef Gürtler (Berlin, 2002), esp. 'Dankbar für manchen klugen Rat', pp. 140–43.

8 *'Schlägt der Äbtissin ein Schnippchen, wählt SPD!' Günter Grass und die Sozialdemokratie*, ed. Kurt Beck (Berlin, 2007).

9 Andreas Kossert, *Kalte Heimat. Die Geschichte der deutschen Vertriebenen nach 1945* (Berlin, 2008), who acknowledges Grass's assistance.

10 'Danger! Being the Log of Captain John Sirius' was published in July 1914 in *The Strand Magazine*.

11 Published in German in 1996.

12 'Introduction: Germany's Memory Contests and the Management of the Past', in *German Memory Contests: The Quest for Identity in Literature, Film and Discourse since 1990*, ed. Anne Fuchs, Mary Cosgrove and Georg Grote (Rochester, NY, 2006), pp. 1–21.

13 This is the conclusion to the travelling exhibition, *Germany's Confrontation with the Holocaust in a Global Context*, curated by Stuart Taberner in 2015. See transnationalholocaustmemory.org.

14 See Jan Knopf, *Die deutsche Kalendergeschichte. Ein Arbeitsbuch* (Frankfurt, 1983).

15 See Harro Zimmermann, *Günter Grass unter den Deutschen. Chronik eines Verhältnisses* (Göttingen, 2006/2010), pp. 571–6.

16 See Stephen Brockmann, 'Die Politik deutschen Leidens. Günter Grass' *Im Krebsgang*', in *Die Wilhelm Gustloff. Geschichte und Erinnerung eines Unterganges*, ed. Bill Niven (Halle, 2011), pp. 285–304.

17 Quoted in 'Shaper of a Nation's Conscience', *The Guardian* (8 March 2003).

8 The Culmination of Project Self

1 This phrase belongs to Stuart Taberner, *Aging and Old-age Style in Günter Grass, Ruth Klüger, Christa Wolf, and Martin Walser: The Mannerism of a Late Period* (Rochester, NY, 2013), p. 43, who also calls the three books 'the autobiographically inspired, genre-bending trilogy', p. 40.

2 Per Øhrgaard, *Günter Grass: Ein Deutscher Schriftsteller wird besichtigt*, trans. Christoph Bartmann (Munich and Vienna, 2005), p. 33.

3 For example, to Heinrich Vormweg, *Günter Grass in Selbstzeugnissen und Bilddokumenten* (Reinbek bei Hamburg, 1986), p. 19.

4 'Am liebsten lüge ich gedruckt', *Der Spiegel* (2 April 1979).

5 *Sechs Jahrzehnte*, pp. 479–81. 'Ich erinnere mich . . .' (2000), XII:578–82.

6 Volker Neuhaus, *Günter Grass. Eine Biographie: Schriftsteller, Künstler, Zeitgenosse* (Göttingen, 2012), pp. 421–2.

7 '"Warum ich nach sechzig Jahren mein Schweigen breche". Günter Grass im Gespräch mit Hubert Spiegel und Frank Schirrmacher', *Frankfurter Allgemeine Zeitung* (11 August 2006). See also Schirrmacher's lead article the following day: 'Das Geständnis' (12 August 2006).

8 Eva Menasse in conversation at the Literaturforum, Brecht-Haus, Berlin, 4 July 2016.

9 *Sechs Jahrzehnte*, pp. 514–16, here p. 515.

10 Peter Oliver Loew, *Danzig: Biographie einer Stadt* (Munich, 2011), pp. 280–81.

11 See Karen Leeder, 'Günter Grass as Poet', in *The Cambridge Companion to Grass*, ed. Taberner, pp. 151–65, esp. pp. 161–2.

12 Stuart Taberner, 'Was gesagt werden muss. Günter Grass's "Israel/Iran Poem of April 2012"', *German Life and Letters* 65:4 (2012), pp. 518–31.

13 Anne Fuchs, *Phantoms of War in Contemporary German Literature, Film, and Discourse: The Politics of Memory* (Rochester, NY, 2008), pp. 172–82.

14 Neuhaus, *Biographie*, p. 428.

15 Grass to Figes, 6 June 1974.

16 Volker Neuhaus, *Günter Grass*, 3rd edn (Stuttgart, 2010), p. 249; *Sechs Jahrzehnte*, p. 538.

17 Updike once said: 'The nearer and dearer they are, the more mercilessly they are served up,' quoted by Adam Begley, *Updike* (New York, 2014), pp. 8–9. His son David said that his father 'decided at an early age that his writing had to take precedence over his relations with real people', ibid., p. 9.

18 Ruth K. Angress, '*Der Butt*: A Feminist Perspective', in *Adventures of a Flounder: Critical Essays on Günter Grass's 'Der Butt'*, ed. Gertrud Bauer Pickar (Munich, 1982), pp. 43–50 (pp. 44–5).

19 Bettina von Arnim, *Die Günderode* (1840); Christa Wolf, *Kein Ort. Nirgends/No Place. Never* (Berlin, 1979).

20 For instance, Gilad Margalit, 'Grass und sein jüdisches alter ego', in *Literarischer Antisemitismus nach Auschwitz*, ed. Klaus Michael Boqdal, Matthias N. Lorenz and Klaus Holz (Stuttgart, 2007), pp. 159–69.

Epilogue: Poetry and Death

1 Grass to Heinz Ludwig Arnold, 19 January 1994.

Select Bibliography

Books by Günter Grass

With the exception of *Grimms Wörter* (Grimms' Words, 2010), Günter Grass's prose oeuvre is readily available in English, translated up to 1992 by Ralph Manheim and since then by Krishna Winston, Breon Mitchell or Michael Henry Heim. Selections of his speeches and essays up to the early 1990s can also be read in English, all published by Secker & Warburg: *Speak Out! Speeches, Open Letters, Commentaries* (1969, trans. Ralph Manheim); *On Writing and Politics, 1967–1983*, with an introduction by Salman Rushdie (1985, trans. Ralph Manheim); *Two States – One Nation?* (1990, trans. Krishna Winston and A. S. Wensinger). *The Günter Grass Reader*, ed. Helmut Frielinghaus (New York, 2004) also contains much valuable material.

There are several collections of Grass's poetry, most recently *Selected Poems: 1956–1993* (London, 1999, trans. Michael Hamburger).

I have referred to the following book titles, arranged here in chronological sequence by publication date. Italicized English titles are available in English translation:

1956: *Die Vorzüge der Windhühner*
       (The Advantages of the Wind Chickens)
1959: *Die Blechtrommel* (*The Tin Drum*)
1960: *Gleisdreieck* (Gleisdreieck)
1961: *Katz und Maus* (*Cat and Mouse*)
1963: *Hundejahre* (*Dog Years*)
1966: *Die Plebejer proben den Aufstand* (*The Plebeians Rehearse the Uprising*)
1967: *Ausgefragt* (Questioned Out)

1968: [and Pavel Kohout], *Briefe über die Grenze. Versuche eines Ost-West Dialoges* (Letters across the Border: Attempts at an East-West Dialogue); [as Artur Knoff], *Geschichten* (Stories)

1969: *Davor* (*Max: A Play*); *Örtlich Betäubt* (*Local Anaesthetic*)

1972: *Aus dem Tagebuch einer Schnecke* (*From the Diary of a Snail*)

1977: *Der Butt* (*The Flounder*)

1979: *Das Treffen in Telgte* (*The Meeting in Telgte*); *Atelier des métamorphoses. Entretiens avec Nicole Casanova* (Studio of Transformation: Conversations with Nicole Casanova)

1980: *Kopfgeburten oder Die Deutschen sterben aus* (*Headbirths, or the Germans are Dying Out*)

1986: *Die Rättin* (*The Rat*)

1988: *Zunge zeigen* (*Show Your Tongue*)

1990: *Totes Holz* (*Dead Wood*)

1991: *Vier Jahrzehnte. Ein Werkstattbericht*, ed. G. Fritz Margull (Four Decades: A Studio Report)

1992: *Unkenrufe* (*The Call of the Toad*)

1993: *Novemberland* (Novemberland)

1995: *Ein weites Feld* (*Too Far Afield*); [and Kenzaboro Oe], *Gestern vor fünfzig Jahren. Ein deutsch-japanischer Briefwechsel* (Yesterday Fifty Years Ago: A German-Japanese Correspondence)

1997: *Fundsachen für Nichtleser* (Lost and Found Items for Non-readers)

1999: *Mein Jahrhundert* (*My Century*); [and Harro Zimmermann], *Vom Abenteuer der Aufklärung* (Of the Adventures of the Enlightenment)

2001: *Fünf Jahrzehnte. Ein Werkstattbericht*, ed. G. Fritz Margull (Five Decades: A Studio Report)

2002: *Im Krebsgang* (*Crabwalk*); [and Daniela Dahn and Johano Strasser, eds), *In einem reichen Land. Zeugnisse alltäglichen Leidens an der Gesellschaft* (In a Rich Country: Witness Statements of Everyday Suffering at the Hands of Society)

2003: *Letzte Tänze* (Last Dances)

2006: *Beim Häuten der Zwiebel* (*Peeling the Onion*)

2007: *Dummer August* (Silly Clown)

2008: *Die Box* (The Box)

2009: *Unterwegs von Deutschland nach Deutschland. Tagebuch 1990* (From Germany to Germany: Diary, 1990)

2010: *Grimms Wörter* (Grimms' Words)

2012: *Eintagsfliegen* (Mayflies)

2014: *Sechs Jahrzehnte. Ein Werkstattbericht*, ed. G. Fritz Margull and Hilke Ohsoling (Six Decades: A Studio Report)

2015: *Vonne Endlichkeit* (*Of All That Ends*)

General Notes on Sources

I quote from the 2007 collected edition published by Steidl, referring to volume and page number. The volumes are as follows: I: *Gedichte und Kurzprosa* (Poetry and Short Prose); II: *Theaterspiele* (Plays); III: *Die Blechtrommel* (The Tin Drum); IV: *Katz und Maus, Hundejahre* (Cat and Mouse, Dog Years); V: *Örtlich Betäubt, Aus dem Tagebuch einer Schnecke* (Local Anaesthetic, From the Diary of a Snail); VI: *Der Butt, Das Treffen in Telgte* (The Flounder, The Meeting in Telgte); VII: *Kopfgeburten oder Die Deutschen sterben aus, Die Rättin, Unkenrufe* (Headbirths, or the Germans are Dying Out, The Rat, The Call of the Toad); VIII: *Ein weites Feld* (Too Far Afield); IX: *Mein Jahrhundert* (My Century); X: *Im Krebsgang, Beim Häuten der Zwiebel* (Crabwalk, Peeling the Onion); XI: *Essays und Reden, 1955–1979*; XII: *Essays und Reden, 1980–2007* (Essays and Speeches).

Unpublished letters are deposited at the Archiv der Akademie der Künste, Berlin. Radio and television sources were accessed at the Medienarchiv Günter Grass Stiftung Bremen held at the Jacobs University.

Angress, Ruth K., '*Der Butt*: A Feminist Perspective', in *Adventures of a Flounder: Critical Essays on Günter Grass's 'Der Butt'*, ed. Gertrud Bauer Pickar (Munich, 1982), pp. 43–50

—, 'A "Jewish Problem" in German Postwar Fiction', *Modern Judaism*, V/3 (1985), pp. 215–33

Arnold, Heinz Ludwig, and Franz Josef Görtz, eds, *Günter Grass. Dokumente zur politischen Wirkung* (Munich, 1971)

Barnert, Arno, 'Eine "herzgraue" Freundschaft. Der Briefwechsel zwischen Paul Celan und Günter Grass', *Textkritische Beiträge*, IX (2004), pp. 65–127

—, Uwe Johnson, Anna Grass, Günter Grass, eds, *Der Briefwechsel* (Frankfurt, 2007)

Baudisch, Julia, '"Und auch Ilsebill war von Anfang an da". Der schönste erste Satz in der Prosa Günter Grass', *Berliner Hefte zur Geschichte des literarischen Lebens* (2013), vol. X, pp. 128–45

Berbig, Roland, 'Das neuste Material in Sachen "Fontane". Dieter Stolz' Korrespondenz mit Günter Grass', *Berliner Hefte zur Geschichte des literarischen Lebens* (2013), vol. X, pp. 83–125

Brady, Philip, Timothy McFarland and John J. White, eds, *Günter Grass's 'Der Butt': Sexual Politics and the Male Myth of History* (Oxford, 1990)

Braun, Rebecca, *Constructing Authorship in the Work of Günter Grass* (Oxford, 2008)

—, and Frank Brunssen, eds, *Changing the Nation: Günter Grass in International Perspective* (Würzburg, 2008)

Brockman, Stephen, 'Die Politik deutschen Leidens. Günter Grass' *Im Krebsgang*', in *Die Wilhelm Gustloff. Geschichte und Erinnerung eines Unterganges*, ed. Bill Niven (Halle, 2011), pp. 285–304

Cosgrove, Mary, *Born under Auschwitz: Melancholy Traditions in Postwar German Literature* (Rochester, NY, 2014)

Detering, Heinrich, and Per Øhrgaard, eds, *Was gesagt wurde. Eine Dokumentation über Günter Grass' 'Was gesagt werden muss' und die deutsche Debatte* (Göttingen, 2013)

Enzensberger, Ulrich, *Die Jahre der Kommune 1. Berlin, 1967–1969* (Cologne, 2004)

Haberkamm, Klaus, 'Verspäteter Grimmelshausen aus der Kaschubei. Verspätete Utopie? Simplicianisches in Grass' "*Der Butt*"', *Simpliciana. Schriften der Grimmelshausen-Gesellschaft*, VI/7 (1985), pp. 123–38

Hall, Katharina, *The 'Danzig Quintet': Explorations in the History and Memory of the Nazi Era from 'Die Blechtrommel' to 'Im Krebsgang'* (Oxford, 2007)

Hermes, Daniela, ed., *Günter Grass/Helen Wolff, Briefe, 1959–1994* (Göttingen, 2003)

—, and Manfred Bissinger, eds, *Zeit sich einzumischen. Die Kontroverse um Günter Grass und die Laudatio auf Yaşar Kemal in der Paulskirche* (Göttingen, 1998)

—, and Oskar Negt, eds, *Der Fall Fonty. 'Ein weites Feld' von Günter Grass im Spiegel der Kritik* (Göttingen, 1996)

Jürgs, Michael, *Bürger Grass. Biografie eines deutschen Dichters* (Munich, 2002/2007/2015)

Kölbel, Martin, ed., *Ein Buch, ein Bekenntnis: Die Debatte um Günter Grass'*
    'Beim Häuten der Zwiebel' (Göttingen, 2007)
—, ed., *Willy Brandt und Günter Grass. Der Briefwechsel* (Göttingen, 2013)
Kossert, Andreas, *Kalte Heimat. Die Geschichte der deutschen Vertriebenen*
    nach 1945 (Berlin, 2008)
Loew, Peter Oliver, *Danzig. Biographie einer Stadt* (Munich, 2011)
Loschütz, Gert, ed., *Von Buch zu Buch. Günter Grass in der Kritik*
    (Darmstadt, 1968)
Magenau, Jörg, *Princeton 66. Die abenteuerliche Reise der Gruppe 47*
    (Stuttgart, 2015)
Mews, Siegfried, *Günter Grass and His Critics: From 'The Tin Drum'*
    to 'Crabwalk' (Rochester, NY, 2008)
Minden, Michael, '"Grass auseinandergeschrieben". Günter Grass's
    Hundejahre and Mimesis', *German Quarterly*, LXXXVI/1 (2013), pp. 25–42
Neuhaus, Volker, *Günter Grass* (Stuttgart, 1979/1993/2010)
—, *Schreiben gegen die verstreichende Zeit. Zu Leben und Werk von Günter Grass*
    (Munich, 1997)
—, *Günter Grass. Eine Biographie: Schriftsteller, Künstler, Zeitgenosse*
    (Göttingen, 2012)
O'Neill, Patrick, 'Musical Form and a Pauline Message in a Key Chapter
    of Grass's *Blechtrommel*', *Seminar*, X (1974), pp. 298–307
Øhrgaard, Per, *Günter Grass. Ein deutscher Schriftsteller wird besichtigt*,
    trans. Christoph Bartmann (Vienna, 2005)
Paver, Chloe, *Narrative and Fantasy in the Post-war German Novel: A Study*
    of Novels by Johnson, Frisch, Wolf, Becker and Grass (Oxford, 1999)
Pezold, Klaus, ed., *Günter Grass. Stimmen aus dem Leseland* (Leipzig, 2003)
Pietsch, Timm Niklas, *'Wer hört noch zu?' Günter Grass als politischer Redner*
    und Essayist (Essen, 2006)
Prawer, S. S., 'The Death of Sigismund Markus: The Jews of Danzig in the
    Fiction of Günter Grass', in *Danzig, between East and West: Aspects of*
    Modern Jewish History, ed. Isadore Twersky (Cambridge, MA, 1985),
    pp. 95–108
Reich-Ranicki, Marcel, *Unser Grass* (Munich, 2003)
Richter, Hans Werner, *Im Etablissement der Schmetterlinge. Einundzwanzig*
    Portraits aus der Gruppe 47 (Munich/Vienna, 1986)
Richter, Sabine, 'Das Kaleidoskop des Günter Grass. Jüdische
    Karikaturen aus der Kaschubei', in *Das literarische und kulturelle Erbe*

von Danzig und Gdańsk, ed. Andrzej Katny (Frankfurt, 2004),
pp. 47–53

Schädlich, Hans Joachim, *Zwischen Schauplatz und Elfenbeinturm*
(Göttingen, 2001)

von Schilling, Klaus, *Schuldmotoren. Artistisches Erzählen in Günter Grass'*
Danziger Trilogie (Bielefeld, 2002)

Schlüter, Kai, *Günter Grass im Visier. Die Stasi-Akte. Eine Dokumentation mit*
Kommentaren von Günter Grass und Zeitzeugen (Berlin, 2010)

——, ed., *Günter Grass auf Tour für Willy Brandt. Die legendäre Wahlkampfreise*
1969 (Berlin, 2011)

Schneider, Gisela, '"Über das Essen, den Nachgeschmack". Studien zum
Motiv des Essens in ausgewählten Werken von Günter Grass', PhD
thesis, National University of Ireland, Cork

Shafi, Monika, ed., *Approaches to Teaching 'The Tin Drum'* (New York, 2008)

Stahl, Enno, *Für die Katz und wider die Maus. Pohlands Film nach Grass*
(Berlin, 2012)

Stolz, Dieter, *Vom privaten Motivkomplex zum epischen Weltentwurf*
(Würzburg, 1994)

——, 'Nomen est omen. *Ein weites Feld* by Günter Grass', in *'Whose Story?' –*
Continuities in Contemporary German-language Literature, ed. Arthur
Williams, Stuart Parkes and Julian Preece (Oxford, 1998), pp. 149–66

——, 'Mein Grass – ein ganz persönlicher Erfahrungsbericht', in
Freipass. Schriften der Günter und Ute Grass Stiftung (2014), vol. i,
pp. 113–36

Taberner, Stuart, ed., *The Cambridge Companion to Günter Grass*
(Cambridge, 2009)

——, 'Was gesagt werden muss. Günter Grass's "Israel/Iran Poem of April
2012"', *German Life and Letters*, lv/4 (2012), pp. 518–31

——, *Aging and Old-age Style in Günter Grass, Ruth Klüger, Christa Wolf,*
and Martin Walser: The Mannerism of a Late Period (Rochester,
ny, 2013)

Tank, Kurt Lothar, *Günter Grass*, trans. John Conway (New York, 1969)

Thomsa, Jörg-Philipp, ed., *Ein Buch schreibt Geschichte. 50 Jahre 'Die*
Blechtrommel' (Lübeck, 2009)

——, and Viktoria Krason, eds, *Von Danzig nach Lübeck. Günter Grass*
und Polen/Z Gdańska do Lubeki. Günter Grass i Polska
(Lübeck/Gdańsk, 2010)

Tighe, Carl, *Gdańsk: National Identity in the Polish-German Borderlands* (London, 1990)

Vormweg, Heinrich, *Günter Grass mit Selbstzeugnissen und Bilddokumenten* (Reinbek bei Hamburg, 1986, 1993, 1996, 1998, 2002)

Weyer, Anselm, and Volker Neuhaus, eds, *Von Katz und Maus und mea culpa. Religiöse Motive im Werk von Günter Grass* (Frankfurt, 2013)

Zimmermann, Harro, *Günter Grass unter den Deutschen. Chronik eines Verhältnisses* (Göttingen, 2006/2010)

Films

Katz und Maus (Cat and Mouse, dir. Hansjürgen Pohland, 1966)

Die Blechtrommel (The Tin Drum, dir. Volker Schlöndorff, 1979)

Die Rättin (The Rat, dir. Martin Buchhorn, 1997)

Unkenrufe. Zeit der Versöhnung (The Call of the Toad: Time of Reconciliation, dir. Robert Glinski, 2004)

Der Unbequeme. Der Dichter Günter Grass (Member of the Awkward Squad: The Poet Günter Grass, dirs Nadja Frenz and Sigrun Matthiesen, 2007)

Spätschicht. Günter Grass bei der Arbeit an Radierungen zu 'Hundejahre' (Late Shift. Günter Grass at Work on the Etchings for *Dog Years*, dir. Sigrun Matthiesen, 2013)

Acknowledgements

This book draws on many years of reading, teaching and writing about Günter Grass. I record my debts to scholars and critics in references but would like also to thank Orlando Figes for sharing his memories of his mother's friendship with Günter Grass; Katie Jones; Volker Neuhaus; Hilke Ohsoling, secretary of the Grass Office in Lübeck; Dieter Stolz; Nicole Thesz; Sonia Wohllaib from the Bremen Medienarchiv; and staff at the Archive in the Akademie der Künste, Berlin, especially Helga Neumann. I owe a special debt to Per Øhrgaard, who kindly read a draft version and offered detailed comments and corrections, from which my manuscript benefited greatly.

For permission to quote from unpublished correspondence held at the Archiv der Akademie der Künste in Berlin, I am grateful also to the Günter and Ute Grass Stiftung, Hans Altenhein, Albrecht Schöne and Gerhard Schröder.

Photo Acknowledgements

The author and publishers wish to express their thanks to the below sources of illustrative material and/or permission to reproduce it:

© Akademie der Künste, Günter Grass Archiv/Sammlung Maria Rama: pp. 19, 20, 23, 38, 39, 41, 42, 186; AKG-images/Niklaus Strauss: p. 6; © Deutsches Literaturarchiv Marbach: p. 78; © Alexander von Hohenthal: p. 180; photo Presse und Informationsamt der Bundesregierung: p. 81; © Heinz Köster/Akademie der Künste/Hans Werner Richter Archiv: p. 84; © Hans Rama/Akademie der Künste, Günter Grass Archiv/Sammlung Maria Rama: pp. 40, 89, 92; © Maria Rama/Akademie der Künste, Günter Grass Archiv/Sammlung Maria Rama: pp. 97, 101, 102, 120, 131; © Toni Richter/Akademie der Künste/Hans Werner Richter Archiv: pp. 45, 96; © Dieter Schmidt/Akademie der Künste/Hans Werner Richter Archiv: pp. 44, 50, 70, 107; © Steidl Verlag/ Günter und Ute Grass Stiftung: p. 108; © Philippa Tuckman (July 2016): p. 93.

kas-acdp, the copyright owner of the image on p. 83, has published it online under conditions imposed by a Creative Commons Attribution-Share Alike 3.0 Germany license; Pelz, the copyright owner of the image on p. 86, has published it online under conditions imposed by a Creative Commons Attribution-Share Alike 3.0 Unported License.

Readers are free:

to share – to copy, distribute and transmit the work
to remix – to adapt the this image alone

Under the following conditions:

attribution – you must attribute the work in the manner specified by the author or licensor (but not in any way that suggests that they endorse you or your use of the work);

share alike – if you alter, transform, or build upon this work, you may distribute the resulting work only under the same or similar license to this one.